BLONDE moments

BLONDE moments

The ditzy gaffes and blunders uttered by blondes of every hue

FLEUR BARRINGTON

MICHAEL O'MARA BOOKS LIMITED

First published in Great Britain in
2008 by Michael O'Mara Books Limited
9 Lion Yard
Tremadoc Road
London SW4 7NQ

A CIP catalogue is available from the British Library

Papers used by Michael O'Mara Books Limited are natural,
recyclable products made from wood grown in sustainable forests.
The manufacturing processes conform to the environmental
regulations of the country of origin.

ISBN: 978-1-84317-311-3

1 3 5 7 9 10 8 6 4 2

Designed and typeset by Ana Bjezancevic

Illustrations by Paul Moran

Printed and bound in Great Britain by Clays Ltd, St Ives plc

www.mombooks.com

'I'm not offended by dumb blonde jokes because I know that I'm not dumb. I also know I'm not blonde.'

DOLLY PARTON

INTRODUCTION

According to *Webster's New Millennium Dictionary of English* a blonde moment is 'an instance of acting dumb or scatterbrained, momentary forgetfulness or ditziness' as in 'Britney Spears was having another blonde moment'. Despite Britney having more than her share of blonde moments, is it true that blondes have more fun as David Hockney infamously claimed, or are they just funnier? The truth is, you don't have to be naturally fair-haired to experience a blonde moment – those times when life jumps up and bites you in embarrassing places, when you wish the earth would open up and swallow you after some daft quip or comment goes wrong. Blonde moments are the things we all say and do when we can't quite synchronize brain, mouth, hands and feet. And you don't have to be a female blonde. There are plenty of male blonds out there too. Take Mayor of London Boris Johnson ('I have as much chance of becoming Prime Minister as of being decapitated by a Frisbee or of finding Elvis') or David Beckham ('I definitely want Brooklyn to be christened, but I don't know into what religion yet').

While senior moments have a common thread of forgetfulness, blonde ones are typified by sudden stupidity, misunderstanding, seeing things from a skewed angle . . . the 'I can't believe I did that' moments when you wonder what you were thinking. They can catch you out at any time: in the car, on the phone, over lunch, walking the kids to school – even during job interviews. Take the driver pulled over by the police for applying make-up while speeding along in her car who attempted to explain it away as 'just a blonde moment' and the woman who wrote in her job application: 'I will give my job my all, so long as it does not interfere with my social life. My social life is very important to me.' Blonde or what?

But for every ditzy blonde there is a clever, powerful, talented one: Margaret Thatcher, Helen Mirren and Madonna all spring to mind, though they too may be permitted the occasional lapse. Talking about her desire to inspire, Madonna quipped: 'I want to be like Gandhi and Martin Luther King and John Lennon . . . but I want to stay alive.'

The world of fashion is one industry that has never baulked at blondeness (in all its forms). In fact, one of the hottest hair trends of recent years – and one that seems to recur every decade or so – is platinum or whiter-than-white blonde. When model *du jour* Agyness Deyn stepped down the catwalks sporting an icy pixie-crop it sparked a trend among celebrities, including Kate Moss, Sophie Dahl and Kylie, for cool platinum locks. According to Gary Richardson of Herbal Essences (who coloured Deyn's hair): 'When someone dyes their hair in such an extreme way, it signals a definite change in the way they feel about themselves. It's a real confidence-booster.'

This book is a celebration of everything blonde, those golden moments from the worlds of art, cinema, politics, sport and more. You'll find quotes and bons mots from an amazing cast, including Victoria Beckham, Marilyn Monroe, Dolly Parton, Dorothy Parker, Hugh Hefner, Boris Johnson and Anna Nicole Smith. There are real accounts of gaffes, blunders and misunderstandings to make you shake your head in disbelief, a fine selection of blonde jokes and a brief history of blondes along with all the latest findings, facts and figures. This is a very special gift for the blonde in your life, be she (or he) natural, bleached or downright brunette. After all, as David Hockney once said, 'If you've only one life, live it as a blonde.'

EARLY BEGINNINGS

The word 'blonde' also has a masculine form: blond. The noun is often used to describe a woman with blonde hair or a fair complexion. 'Blonde' made its first appearance in the English dictionary in 1481 and comes from the old French *blont*, meaning 'a colour midway between golden and light chestnut'.

'Blonde' remains one of the few adjectives with separate masculine and feminine forms. Blond/e (spelled either way) is also used to describe soft furnishings, pale woods and even lager, while 'blonde lace', originally of unbleached cream-coloured Chinese silk, was once used to edge French pillowcases.

'What good are vitamins? Eat four lobsters, eat a pound of caviar – live! If you are in love with a beautiful blonde with an empty face and no brain at all, don't be afraid, marry her – live!'
ARTUR RUBINSTEIN, POLISH PIANIST (1887–1982)

BEAUTY SCHOOL DROPOUT

In the final round of Miss Teen America 2007, Miss South Carolina was asked why she thought a fifth of Americans were unable to locate the United States on a world map. She had what can only be described as a moment of catastrophic blondeness as, unable to answer the question, she blustered bravely on:

'I personally believe that US Americans are unable to do so because, er, some people out there in our nation don't have maps, and I believe that our education, like such as in South Africa and the Iraq, everywhere like . . . such as. And I believe that they should . . . our education over here in the US should help the US, er, should help South Africa and should help the Iraq and the Asian countries so we will be able to build up our future for our children.'

Right . . .

PLATINUM BLONDE = DUMB?

It seems both men and women believe in the stereotypical dumb blonde. Psychologists have found that many people consider hair colour to be associated with certain personality characteristics. Dr Tony Cassidy and Georgina Harris of the University of Coventry asked 120 people (sixty men and sixty women) to look at photos of a female model wearing four different wigs: platinum blonde, natural-looking blonde, brown and red. Subjects were asked to rate the model for popularity, intelligence, shyness, aggressiveness and temperament.

At the British Psychological Society's annual conference in Belfast the researchers presented their results. The platinum blonde was rated less intelligent, particularly by men, while the brown-haired model was assumed to be shyer, and the natural blonde more popular. Dr Cassidy reported, 'It seems that the stereotype about dumb blondes did exist, but only in terms of the platinum blonde.' The natural blonde was not regarded as 'dumb' but was given the highest popularity rating.

Admitting he was surprised at the findings, Dr Cassidy said, 'It's important to understand that we do make judgements based on stereotypes and if we make judgements that have important implications for the people we are judging, we need to be aware of this situation. It's quite likely that the people who rated this individual less intelligent were not actually aware that they were doing it, which is frightening.'

But he could not explain why the 'dumb' label was attached to the platinum, but not the natural blonde. 'I suspect that the stereotype is probably stronger in men than in women,' he said. He went on to say that he thought the idea of the 'dumb blonde' probably emerged with the development of films, TV and glossy magazines.

HITCHHIKER'S HELL

A blonde cleaner thanked the lorry driver who dropped her off at the supermarket where she worked, but failed to notice he had in fact dropped her off at the wrong branch. She was not just in the wrong town but the wrong country. She arrived in Tartu, Estonia, over three hundred miles from her own branch in Kaunas, Lithuania, following a mix-up in translation.

I might be a dumb blonde but
I am good at speling.

BEVY OF BLONDES

At the 2006 Allan Border Medal cricket function in Australia, the players were almost out-shadowed by their wives or girlfriends. Apart from one lonely brunette, they all had long blonde hair, big white smiles, deep tans and plenty of cleavage on display. What was going on? Dr John Armstrong, associate professor of philosophy at the University of Melbourne and author of *The Secret Power of Beauty*, was of the view that Sigmund Freud would conclude they were all the same woman.

'The men are bonding by having one woman who they share between them,' Dr Armstrong revealed, going on to describe them as 'normopaths . . . people who are pathologically determined to be like other people, to have the same kind of things.' Blondeness and its eternal allure is all to do with lustre because, he explained, 'human beings go for things with a sheen to them.'

'I'm getting more famouser by the day.'
AVRIL LAVIGNE

GENTLEMEN DON'T ALWAYS PREFER BLONDES

Researchers at City University, London conducted a survey to assess the stereotypes attached to different hair colour in women. They showed 1500 men three photos of the same model, digitally enhanced as a blonde, brunette and redhead. The men then attempted to outline the personality of each 'model'. Eighty-one per cent of the men described the brunette as 'intelligent', while 67 per cent considered her 'independent and 'self-sufficient'. The brunette was regarded as 'stable' and 'competent', by 62 per cent, while 40 per cent thought the blonde 'needy' and 'lacking in independence'. The redheads fared better, with 79 per cent of men thinking her 'intelligent', although another 45 per cent were convinced she was 'neurotic'.

Professor of psychology Peter Ayrton, who led the research, said that blonde hair had always been seen as a symbol of youth, which was attractive to men, adding, 'As the role of women has evolved, men's expectations of women have changed. They're looking for more intense, equal partnerships and appearance has a large role to play.'

'It isn't that gentlemen really prefer blondes, it's just that we look dumber.'
ANITA LOOS, FROM *GENTLEMEN PREFER BLONDES*

CUTTING EDGE

A chef working at a hotel in Switzerland managed to lose a finger in a meat-cutting machine and after a little hopping around, he submitted an insurance claim. Suspecting negligence, the company sent a representative out to take a look. He tried the machine out – and lost a finger. The chef's claim was approved, leaving the insurance company looking a little sheepish.

'I can't go more than seventy-two hours without shopping, but I don't think I'm excessive.'
HILARY DUFF

AN ENDANGERED SPECIES?

Blonde hair is caused by a recessive gene: for a child to be born blonde, the gene must be present on both sides of the family in the grandparents' generation.

A hoax study by 'experts' in Germany in 2002 predicted that by 2202 blondes would become extinct. So-called 'bottle' blondes were to blame for the demise of the natural blonde, said the bogus researchers. They claimed dyed blondes are more attractive to men, who choose them as partners over natural blondes.

*

A blonde was on a tour of a national park. The park warden mentioned to the tour group that dinosaur fossils had been found in the area. 'Wow!' the blonde exclaimed, 'I can't believe dinosaurs would come this close to the motorway!'

BAD HAIR DAY

This phrase was coined to describe a day when nothing seems to be going right – including your hair. To wit:

> 'I'm fine but you're obviously having
> a bad hair day.'
> BUFFY TO THE ONE-ARMED VAMPIRE AMILYN,
> *BUFFY THE VAMPIRE SLAYER* (1992)

MADNESS IN THE MIDDLE AGES

The blond Vikings of Sweden, Norway and Denmark settled in many of the countries they invaded, including England, and subsequently many of their words entered the language, including the phrase 'to go berserk' – possibly one of the earliest examples of an extreme 'blonde moment'.

In Old Norse, the word 'berserk' means 'bear shirt' and Viking warriors (or 'berserkers') donned bearskins as opposed to body armour to make them feel crazy as a bear in anticipation of battle. They overran and terrorized England and Northern Europe, often assisted along the way by hallucinogenic mushrooms. The earliest king of Norway, Harald Fairhair (AD 850–933) had berserkers as his household guard.

'I'm getting a trainer. But not to lose anything – because I like being a little thicker.'
CHRISTINA AGUILLERA

A THOUSAND SHIPS

In Greek mythology, blonde beauty Helen of Troy was the daughter of Leda and Zeus. Her loveliness was so overwhelming that Theseus once abducted her and she had to be rescued by her loyal brothers. In order to prevent feuds and discord, Helen's father made it a condition for all her many suitors that they should unite behind whoever was chosen as her husband.

Helen eventually married Menelaus, the future King of Sparta. When Paris of Troy abducted her, Menelaus's former rivals were forced to honour their oath and bring her back home and so began the Trojan War.

An apparition of Helen appears briefly in Christopher Marlowe's *Faustus*, prompting the immortal line, 'Is this the face that launched a thousand ships?', which was satirized in the film *Shakespeare in Love*.

'The reason that the all-American boy prefers beauty to brains is that he can see better than he can think.'
FARRAH FAWCETT

GOING BACK TO YOUR ROOTS

The use of blonde washes is recorded in Pliny's letters during the early Roman Empire. The Romans were so impressed with the hair of their slaves from Northern Europe that they decided to create their own bleaching lotion: a mixture of rock alum, quicklime, elderberries, nutshells and wood ash, combined with dregs of wine. This 'blonde wash' was left on for several days until their hair turned a reddish-gold – a far cry from buying a sachet from the chemist.

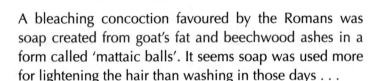

When in the sixth century Pope Gregory the Great first encountered blond, blue-eyed English boys at a slave market, he remarked, 'Non Angli sed Angeli' – 'Not Angles but Angels' – surely one of the loveliest blonde moments in history.

A bleaching concoction favoured by the Romans was soap created from goat's fat and beechwood ashes in a form called 'mattaic balls'. It seems soap was used more for lightening the hair than washing in those days . . .

A later report by a Dr Marinello of Modena, Italy in 1562 records that mixtures of alum, black sulphur and honey were commonly used for bleaching. However, it was a combination of components that not only caused the hair to fall out but also seriously damaged the complexion. 'Permit me to remind you, honoured and honourable ladies,' he wrote, 'that the application of so many colours to your hair may strike a chill into the head like the shock of a shower-bath, that it affects and penetrates and, what is worse, may entail divers grave maladies and infirmities; therefore I should advise you to take all possible precautions.' Quite what those precautions might have been is left unsaid.

'As for blondes having more fun, well, let me dispel that rumour forever. They do.'

MAUREEN LIPMAN

CHEMISTRY CLASS

$_2H_2O + _{20}H_2O$ = the chemical process for bleaching

Thenard first discovered hydrogen peroxide in 1818 but its cosmetic application didn't really take off until 1867 when it was promoted by pharmacist and perfumer E. H. Thiellay and Leon Hugo, a hairdresser in the Paris Exposition. Using a 3 per cent solution of hydrogen peroxide under the trade name 'Eau de fontaine de jouvence golden', they demonstrated its bleaching effect on hair. This quickly became popular in the US and Europe.

'Even I don't wake up looking
like Cindy Crawford.'
CINDY CRAWFORD

TOP HIGHLIGHTING TIPS

* Adding colour to fine hair gives extra body because colouring causes the shafts of the hair to swell.

* Highlights around the face brighten the complexion. Colours will warm the skin and enhance natural hair colour.

* Ask your stylist about lowlights: create depth and drama by weaving darker strands into lighter ones.

* Traditional foil highlights are harder to care for once your roots grow out. Precise application is necessary, which means fixing dark roots can be pricey. Widely spaced, less structured colour is easier for touch-ups.

* Choose full or partial highlights. With partial highlights the stylist adds colour to the top of the head instead of highlighting all over. For thick hair, go partial otherwise you'll be there for hours!

* If you do opt for partial highlights, in the summer ask your stylist to colour the hair that shows when you wear a ponytail.

* Afterwards, use a colour-preserving shampoo and keep your hair moisturized with regular applications of conditioner.

'Don't overstyle your hair. Let it dry naturally sometimes and always use a wide-toothed comb. Buy shampoo for blonde hair and use a treatment instead of a regular conditioner. Lavender shampoos prevent hair looking brassy. Treat hair to a mask once a week. If your hair's fine, try an oil-based mask, otherwise opt for a rich cream.'

NICOLA CLARKE, CREATIVE COLOUR DIRECTOR AT JOHN FRIEDA

BLONDE, SEVENTIES-STYLE

Popular pin-up of the 1970s Farrah Fawcett-Majors starred as private detective Jill Munroe alongside Kate Jackson and Jaclyn Smith as one of the 'three little girls' in the television series *Charlie's Angels*. Men were not the only admirers of her tousled, 'dirty-blonde' tresses – women across the world adopted her feather-blown hairstyle. Long curly locks were held in place with an abundance of hairspray, typifying the seventies. That hair was to prove dangerous, however. Her former husband, actor Lee Majors (the *Six Million Dollar Man*) once claimed that he suffered a broken nose as a result of Farrah rolling over in her sleep, her rock-solid hair striking his face.

CUPPING CATASTROPHE

In 2004 actress Gwyneth Paltrow caused a stir by stepping out to a New York preview in a low-cut top and revealing a back covered in large circular bruises that appeared to be love-bites or even welts.

Gwyneth had had a 'cupping' session, a kind of acupuncture practised for thousands of years. Heated cups are placed over the skin to encourage blood flow and ease stress, aches and pains. Paltrow admitted she was too busy trying to disguise her post-pregnancy tummy to consider the enormous burn-marks on her back: 'I'm such an idiot sometimes. I have been a big fan of Chinese medicine for a long time because it works and it's thousands of years old.'

While the process was 'amazing', she completely forgot about it when dressing to go out. 'When I got back in the car at the end of the evening and turned to Jenny, my assistant, and I said, "Oh my gosh, I just realized I have these things and I think people are going to . . ." She was like, "Oh please . . . who do you think you are? Get over it!" And then it was on the cover of the *New York Post*.'

BABY BLONDE

Blonde hair is common in babies and children, so much so that 'baby blonde' has been coined to mean very fair hair. Blonde hair also tends to darken with age and often hair that is blonde in childhood becomes light to dark brown in adolescence.

Some scientists believe this is to do with pigmentation. A lot of eumelanin in the skin and hair gives a baby dark hair, while a small amount produces blonde hair. Hair colour is not necessarily a dominant gene, which is why a baby may have different hair colour to his parents, or even siblings. The same applies to texture.

'Sometimes I feel that there's a baby inside me that hasn't grown up yet. So Shakira can be a very confusing character.'
SHAKIRA, POP SOLO ARTIST

IT'S A QUESTION OF STYLE

According to celebrity stylist and doyenne of hair colour Jo Hansford, all blondes should buy themselves a water filter 'because hard water means you'll have to use even more conditioner'.

Millie Kendall of make-up company Ruby & Millie is 'naturally an artificial blonde' and recommends tinting your roots every three weeks. She says, 'My only rule about blonde hair is no red lipstick – it just looks trashy, especially with dark roots. Oh, and use loads of cheek colour – you want to look like a young blonde, not an old one.'

Dark eyebrows can be as much of a giveaway as non-blonde hair 'down there' (witness James Bond's quip about blondes and brunettes in *Diamonds are Forever*). If you want to go blonde all over, use cream bleach (with care and only after a patch test) to bleach your brows for an extreme sixties look. If your blonde hair is fading, take solace in heat-accelerated highlighting gels for retouching roots and highlighting all shades of blonde. They work in sunshine or under the heat of a hairdryer.

'When choosing between two evils, I always like to try the one I've never tried before.'
MAE WEST

CLARKSON'S BLONDE MOMENT

In a typically testosterone-fuelled stunt, *Top Gear*'s Jeremy Clarkson decided to pit a Jaguar S-Type diesel against the formidable Nurburgring race track in Germany in 2004 – and complete the circuit in less than ten minutes.

After numerous attempts he finally made it by a hair's breadth. When fellow presenter Richard Hammond (aka The Hamster) joked that it was so close it was a bit 'Hollywood', Clarkson's race tutor, flaxen-haired Sabine Schmitz, laughed. She then proceeded to take the car for a single spin round the track – returning to a crestfallen Clarkson in 9 minutes 12 seconds. A year later she very nearly beat his record again – this time in a Ford Transit van.

And finally, in series eleven of *Top Gear* she beat him in a double-decker car race on the Zolder circuit in Belgium.

NATURAL WOMAN

While natural dyes using lemon juice or camomile are not as potent as colouring agents, they are a great way to subtly change the colour of your hair. You may have to use them over a period of time to build up to your desired shade – and always remember to do a strand test first to see if you like the look.

Lemon

Apply the juice of two lemons to your hair. If time and the weather allow, lie in the sun. Otherwise apply heat from a hairdryer until your hair has lightened to the required shade.

Camomile

Fading blonde locks can be noticeably brightened with this herb. For a camomile rinse, add 250ml camomile flowers to a litre of boiling water. Boil for 40 minutes, then allow to cool. Meanwhile, wash your hair. Strain the camomile mixture and pour through your hair after towel-drying, catching the run-off in a bowl. Pour through several more times. Leave for 20 minutes before rinsing your hair. Apply twice a week for maximum brightness.

DEGREES OF BLONDE

* *Ash blonde*: mostly fair, with some grey tones.

* *Bleached (bottled) blonde*: artificially dyed blonde hair.

* *Brownish blonde*: the kindest way to describe mousey, really. The darkest shade of blonde, sometimes light brown, other times dark blonde.

* *Dirty blonde*: not as exciting as it sounds, this is dark blonde. Also known as dishwasher blonde.

* *Golden (or honey) blonde*: lighter blonde, with a warm golden cast.

* *Hazy (or zebra) blonde*: hair that is streaked blonde and brunette.

* *Platinum blonde*: think Marilyn Monroe or Jean Harlow; almost white and found naturally in children but rare among adults.

* *Pool blonde*: blonde with green undertones from regular exposure to chlorinated water. (Rinse and condition thoroughly after swimming!)

* *Sandy blonde*: fair, slightly rusty-looking . . . a little nondescript, perhaps.

* *Strawberry blonde*: reddish blonde. (A friend of mine witnessed an interesting exchange between a raging drunk and a policeman on the streets of Oxford. Drunk: 'Leave me alone, you ginger knob b*****d!' Copper: 'How dare you! I'm strawberry blond and you're under arrest.')

* *Sunny blonde*: Doris Day blonde – very bright, almost light yellow to yellow.

'When it comes to spotting a blonde hair on a man's coat, every wife has 20-20 vision.'
REESE WITHERSPOON AS ELLE WOODS IN
LEGALLY BLONDE (2001)

ROLLING STONE

In early 2008 West Country girl Joss Stone gave journalists at a fundraiser her unique take on the relative values of loose tobacco and cigarettes. 'In England we smoke rolled cigarettes. It's better to smoke rollies than straights because straights have chemicals that keep them burning. So if you really have to smoke, smoke rollies.'

The US National Heart, Lung and Blood Institute, whose charity event she was attending at the time, must have been thrilled (especially as hand-rolled cigarettes are in fact *more* carcinogenic).

> 'Smoking kills. If you're killed, you've lost a very important part of your life.'
> BROOKE SHIELDS

LANDSLIDE

Another recent example of a celeb cutting loose from their publicist and making a startlingly crazy comment comes from Sharon Stone. She suggested the earthquakes that hit China's Sichuan province in May 2008, causing an estimated 70,000 deaths, were down to 'bad karma'. Speaking at the Cannes Film Festival the actress mused, 'I'm, you know, not happy about the way the Chinese are treating the Tibetans, because I don't think anyone should be unkind to anyone else. And so I have been very concerned about how to think and what to do about that, because I don't like that. And then I've been concerned about, oh, how should we deal with the Olympics, because they're not being nice to the Dalai Lama, who is a good friend of mine. And then all this earthquake and all this stuff happened and I thought, "Is that karma? When you're not nice bad things happen to you?"'

DID YOU KNOW?

* Jean Harlow's famous platinum locks regularly broke off because she anointed them with a mix of household bleach, hydrogen peroxide, soap flakes and ammonia. With her hair taking a constant battering in the cause of art, she was eventually forced to wear a wig.

* In 2005 American scientists at the Mayo Clinic and Johns Hopkins University discovered that blondes have nearly 380 per cent more sex (of all kinds) than those with hair of any other hue. But the study also showed that they only achieved orgasm at a rate on par with other colours and they faked orgasm at least eight times as often. 'This is significant,' said psychologist Dr Ruth Hathaway. 'It tells us that the blonde is willing to sacrifice her pleasure for the sexual gratification of her partner, something that is seen to be a bit more "stingy", if you will, in other hair colours.'

* A major British food chain reports that blonde cashiers attract more clients to their cash registers than brunettes.

* More cheer for blondes: brunettes are usually the first to get grey hair!

* In the States, an online dating service revealed that blondes get 30 per cent more messages than redheads and 10 per cent more than brunettes. In fact, blondes are still more popular even for profiles without pictures.

* Miss Snively, head of the Blue Book School of Charm and Modelling, told Marilyn Monroe to bleach her hair and cut a quarter of an inch off one of her high heels to give her that famous wiggle.

* In Elizabethan times, inspired by their elegant queen, women used a mix of powdered silver and pigeon dung to bleach their hair: revolting – and hugely expensive.

THE 'IDEAL' WOMAN

In a 2008 survey of 66,000 male members of top dating site ukdating.com, it was revealed that most men would like to come home to a pretty 5'8" blue-eyed blonde who is good in bed and doesn't earn too much. So much for gender stereotyping! Here is the list of their top fifteen attributes:

1. Blue eyes
2. Long blonde hair
3. Occasionally wears glasses
4. Height of 5'8"
5. Weighs about 9.5 stone
6. A size 12
7. Good in bed
8. Earns less than £25,000 a year
9. Extremely fit
10. Very good-looking
11. Wacky personality
12. Rents a house or flat
13. Optimistic
14. Owns a Ford Ka or Mazda MX5
15. Works as a nurse or PR executive

THE WORLD OF BARBIE

With physical proportions unlike those of any woman on the planet, Barbie is not a politically correct toy by any stretch of the imagination. While you won't find a Hillary Clinton or a Judi Dench Barbie, a platinum blonde Marilyn and a Cher in her signature Bob Mackie gown are just two models of the toy described by its manufacturers as 'More than a doll'.

The marketing execs were more apt than they'd realized. In fact, the government of Iran regards Barbie as one of the most insidious weapons of Western culture – however, in spite of several attempts to boycott imports, Barbie remains one of the highest selling toys in the region.

'You know you've made it when you've been moulded in miniature plastic. But you know what children do with Barbie dolls . . . it's a bit scary, actually.'
CATE BLANCHETT

LIGHT BLOND ANNIVERSARY

To mark one hundred years in the teddy-making business Steiff launched the '100 Years Anniversary Bear Light Blond LE 2002', as part of a set of three different coloured bears. It was made in light blonde, straight pile mohair with matching wool felt pads, soft brown eyes and a brown stitched nose. Each one came with a porcelain medal on a red ribbon, numbered swing certificate, white tag no. 671043 and the all-important Steiff button.

WEIRD SCIENCE

'Being a Scientologist, when you drive past an accident you know you have to do something about it because you know you're the only one that can really help.'
TOM CRUISE

'[Tom Cruise] is a good person. I think he gets a raw deal, just as I think the orphans in Malawi get a raw deal; just as I think a lot of marginalized people get a raw deal.'
MADONNA

'Tom has – we all have – the right to practice how we feel. Don't judge someone until they have tossed your salad.'
JOHN TRAVOLTA

BLONDE BABY CRISIS

Cryos International, a sperm bank in New York that specializes in imported goods, reported that supplies were running, ahem, dry towards the end of 2007. Sperm samples from thirty countries were banned by the Food and Drug Administration (FDA) in the States to prevent the spread of Creutzfeldt-Jakob disease.

New Yorkers desperate to have a fashionably blue-eyed, blond baby were dismayed to learn that offerings from fair-haired Scandinavians had apparently gone to, er, seed. 'We have a waiting list of fifteen to twenty couples,' reported sperm-bank manager Claus Rodgaard. He confirmed that most of the Northern European supplies would be gone by 2008.

The FDA preferred not to comment, but cited the conclusions of a 2001 committee finding that CJD could be passed through sperm. 'I'd rather take the chance and end up with another perfect child,' said one determined Manhattan mother.

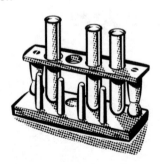

'Fame is also a test of character at times . . .
Sometimes I pass the test, sometimes I'm a pain
in the ass. Sometimes I'm like, "Oh, God! I just
want to buy some tampons!"'
MEG RYAN

BLONDE JOKES . . .

A blonde was bragging about her knowledge of European capitals. She said to her friend proudly, 'Go ahead and ask me, I know all of them.' Her friend replies, 'Okay, what's the capital of Luxembourg?' 'Oh that's easy,' she replies. 'L!'

*

A famous football player parks his brand new Porsche outside a designer clothes store and goes inside to shop. About ten minutes later a blonde saleswoman runs up to him, shouting, 'I just saw someone steal your car!' 'Did you try to stop him?' he asks. 'No,' replies the blonde. 'I did much better than that – I got the registration number!'

*

A blonde ordered a pizza and the waiter asked if he should cut it into six or twelve pieces. 'Six, please. I could never eat twelve!' she replied.

*

Another blonde calls her boyfriend and says, 'Please come over and help me . . . I have a really hard jigsaw puzzle and I just can't figure out how to get started.' Her boyfriend asks, 'What's it meant to be when it's finished?' The blonde says, 'According to the picture on the box, it's a tiger.' Her boyfriend decides to go over and help. She lets him in and shows him the puzzle. He studies the pieces for a while, then looks at the box and turns to her and says, 'Well, first of all, we're not going to be able to assemble these pieces into anything resembling a tiger.' He holds her hand, smiles sweetly and continues, 'Relax, let's have a cup of coffee and then . . . let's put the frosted flakes back in the box.'

LITERARY CRITIC

Boris Johnson once sat on a panel for the BBC's *Question Time* when the question was posed: 'Is Salman Rushdie's knighthood an insult to Muslims worldwide?' In response, the Tory MP said that he objected to the knighthood on 'purely literary grounds', having struggled with Rushdie's 'impenetrable' books. In his view Dick Francis had 'a better grasp of pace and character and plot'.

LIMERICK TIME

A blonde-haired young lady from Wales
Applied for a job tracking sales.
When they asked, 'Can you file?'
She proceeded to smile
And held up ten pretty red nails.

Once a sleepy blonde waitress, Liz Dower
Dreamt she was taking a shower.
When she woke she construed
She was totally nude
But she made some good tips that half hour!

I once met an extremely sad lady
Who confessed, 'When the world's dark and shady
And my prospects look thin
I think nothing and grin
And pretend that I'm blonde and named Brady.'

THE BARBIE BANDITS

In 2007, two nineteen-year-old blondes, Heather Johnston and Ashley Miller, created a sensation throughout the USA. Dubbed the 'Barbie Bandits', they stole roughly $11,000 from the Bank of America in the small town of Acworth, Georgia. Heather had won a scholarship and was studying in the first year of college; she was also a rising tennis player but it seems she had an appetite for fast money and luxury goods. To finance her lifestyle, she started a night-job erotic strip dancing in a nightclub, where she could earn nearly $1,000 in a few days. When Heather's parents confronted her about her new job, she left home.

It was at the nightclub that she met fellow stripper Ashley Miller. Heather, Ashley and Ashley's boyfriend, Michael Chastang, became friends. One February night in 2007, the girls joked with Michael about robbing a bank. The next day, Michael told Heather that he knew a bank clerk, 22-year-old Herman Allen, who was happy to be their linkman. Accordingly, Heather contacted Herman, who guided her precisely in what to write on the note she was to slip to the specific teller counter.

Clad in trendy outfits, the girls headed towards the bank. But they went to the wrong branch. After contacting their linkman, they proceeded to the right one. At the counter, they handed over the note containing threatening language and the teller immediately began to throw cash in the air. The girls were so engrossed in collecting money in their bags that they completely forgot about CCTV. Leaving in a hurry, the Barbie Bandits first went to their apartment, where they divided the cash into four bundles for themselves, Michael and Herman. From there, they visited a mall and purchased whatever caught their eye and then paid a visit to Atlanta's priciest hair salon, where they were again caught on CCTV having their hair done.

Police broadcasted the bank surveillance photos on TV throughout the US and soon they were arrested. The dream was over: Heather Johnston spent a month in prison and was sentenced to ten years probation, while Ashley Miller is serving two years of the maximum ten-year jail sentence.

'Nobody deserves to be treated like a princess
one hundred per cent of the time . . .
not even me.'
JESSICA SIMPSON

FREQUENTLY ASKED QUESTIONS

Q: Why do blondes like lightning?
A: They think someone's taking their picture.

Q: Why did the blonde get so excited when she finished
   her jigsaw puzzle in only six months?
A: Because the box said: 'From 2 to 4 years'.

Q: Why do blondes drive BMWs?
A: Because they can spell it.

Q: When a blonde dyes her hair brunette, what do you
   call it?
A: Artificial Intelligence.

Q: Why didn't the blonde have ice cubes at her party?
A: She lost the recipe.

Q: So, what's the difference between a clever blonde
   and a UFO?
A: People have actually seen UFOs.

Q: How do you know if your girlfriend is a natural
   blonde?
A: Blow in her ear and if she's a true blonde she'll
   start to float.

THE NEW MALE BLOND

According to some scientists at Nanterre University in Paris, it seems the 'dumb blonde' stereotype is so firmly planted in the male psyche that men subconsciously become more foolish than they really are whenever they meet a blonde. Now, 'blonde' has long been a byword for women not overly blessed when it comes to intellect, but this research has been carried out to see whether many wives and girlfriends who have witnessed their men acting foolishly in the company of a blonde stranger have a right to be concerned.

Men were shown photos of women with different coloured hair then asked to take a general knowledge test. Those shown photos of blondes scored lower marks than men who looked at brunettes or redheads. Without realizing it, they mimic what they believe, incorrectly, to be the lesser intelligence of the blonde to get along with her, or so the scientists suggest.

Professor Thierry Meyer, the study joint author concluded: 'It proves that people confronted with stereotypes generally behave in line with them. Blondes have the potential to make people act in a dumber way because they mimic the unconscious stereotype of the dumb blonde.'

'It's a pain in the ass. I never thought I would ever use terms like "my roots" Or "my dye job" or "my colour's not holding!"'

FREDDIE PRINZE JR ON GOING BLOND FOR THE FILM *SCOOBY DOO*

EVOLUTIONARY EVIDENCE

According to anthropologists at St Andrews University, Northern European women evolved blue eyes and blonde hair through sexual selection at the end of the Ice Age. Blondes stood out more from their darker rivals at a time when males were scarce and competition for them particularly fierce.

Some psychologists have also suggested that because white babies are often born blond, there is a primal link between childhood and blondeness, encouraging people to admire and fawn over the fair-haired.

'Since I had the baby I can't tolerate anything
violent or sad. I saw *The Matrix* and I had
my eyes closed through a lot of it, though
I didn't need to. I would peek and then think,
oh, OK, I can see that!'

LISA KUDROW AKA PHOEBE FROM *FRIENDS*

GORGEOUS GEORGE

When blue-eyed MP for Bethnal Green and Bow George Galloway made the momentous decision to appear on *Celebrity Big Brother 4* perhaps the nation wasn't quite ready to witness him in all his glory. On entrance to the *Big Brother* house, he proclaimed, 'I believe that politicians should use every opportunity to communicate with people.' Quite what he was attempting to get across when he put on a skintight red catsuit and attempted a robot dance with fellow contestant Pete Burns, we'll never know. Other disastrous highlights of his short-lived *BB* tenure include being called a 'naughty pussycat' and pretending to lick milk from Rula Lenska's lap, dressing up as a vampire and squabbling with Michael Barrymore over cigars.

FINANCIAL UNCERTAINTY

In early 2008 a viewer emailed *Mad Money*, an American cable TV programme on CNBC, to ask financial pundit Jim Cramer, 'Should I be worried about Bear Stearns in terms of liquidity and get my money out of there?' Cramer replied 'NO! NO! NO! Bear Stearns is fine! Do not take your money out! Bear Stearns is not in trouble, I mean if anything they're likely to get taken over. Don't move your money from Bear – that's just being SILLY! Don't be SILLY!' Six days later Bear Stearns shares crashed to $2 each and Cramer's rant rocketed to the top of YouTube.com.

'I'm blonde. What's your excuse?'
REESE WITHERSPOON AS ELLE WOODS IN *LEGALLY BLONDE*

NO LOVE LOST

Brigitte Bardot revealed her true stance on female solidarity after a grease fire took hold in her kitchen. A female friend set forth in an attempt to do battle with the flames. Bardot, meanwhile, fled the room and slammed the door, trapping her friend inside. Bardot's husband at once intervened and was stunned by her reasoning: 'If I open the door,' she explained, 'all my furniture will go up in flames!'

NOT SO DUMB . . .

Despite hotel heiress Paris Hilton being dubbed the 'heir-head' there is no scientific evidence that blondes are less intelligent than their dark-haired counterparts, and many blondes belie the dumb blonde image. Marilyn Monroe is said to have possessed an IQ of 170 (easily above the minimum required to be a Mensa member) and once quipped, 'I can be smart when it's important but most men don't like it.' Equally smart *Absolutely Fabulous* actress Joanna Lumley is a noted environmentalist and a fellow of the Royal Geographical Society.

Not only do blondes have more fun, they also have more hair on their heads than brunettes. Approximately 140,000 compared with 108,000 for their dark-haired friends.

TRAVELLING LIGHT

A blonde is sitting next to a man on an aeroplane. About an hour into the flight, the pilot says over the intercom, 'One of our four engines is out. We will be about fifteen minutes late arriving.' Thirty minutes later, he comes on the intercom again and says, 'There's a second engine out. We'll be another thirty minutes late.' Fifteen minutes later, he announces, 'I'm sorry to say there's a third engine out and we'll be about an hour late arriving at our destination.' The blonde turns to the man beside her and says, 'Man, if that fourth engine goes out, we'll be up here all day!'

A blonde calls up an airline ticket counter and asks, 'How long are your flights from London to LA?' The person manning the desk replies, 'Just a minute.' She thanks him and hangs up.

A plane is on its way to Melbourne when a blonde in economy class gets up and moves to the first-class section and sits down. The flight attendant watches her do this and asks to see her ticket. She then tells the blonde that, as she's paid for an economy seat, she'll have to go and sit in the back. The blonde replies, 'I'm blonde, I'm beautiful, I'm going to Melbourne and I'm staying right here!'

The flight attendant enters the cockpit and tells the pilot and co-pilot there's a woman sitting in first class who belongs in economy and she won't go back to her seat. The co-pilot goes back to the blonde and tries to explain. The blonde replies, 'I'm blonde, I'm beautiful, I'm going to Melbourne and I'm staying right here!'

Exasperated, the co-pilot tells his pilot that it's no use and that he should probably have the police waiting when they land to arrest the blonde who won't listen to reason. But the pilot responds, 'You say she's *blonde*? I'll handle this. I'm married to a blonde and I speak blonde!' He goes back to the blonde, whispers in her ear and she says, 'I'm sorry, I had no idea,' gets up and returns to her original seat. The flight attendant and co-pilot are amazed and ask what he said to make her move without fuss. The pilot replied, 'I told her first class isn't going to Melbourne!'

POP GEOGRAPHY

'I love being in America.'
CHARLOTTE CHURCH, WHILE VISITING TORONTO

'So, where's the Cannes Film Festival
being held this year?'
CHRISTINA AGUILLERA

'The cool thing about being famous
is travelling. I have always wanted
to travel across seas - like to Canada
and stuff.'
BRITNEY SPEARS

'I'm not anorexic. I'm from Texas.
Are there people from Texas that are
anorexic? I've never heard of one.
And that includes me.'
JESSICA SIMPSON

'I've never really wanted to go to Japan.
Simply because I don't like eating fish.
And I know that's very popular out
there in Africa.'
BRITNEY SPEARS

'I was in geography class and the teacher said to raise your hand if you know the continents. I raised my hand and said, "A, E, I, O, U." And the teacher replied, "Those aren't even consonants. They're vowels!"'
JESSICA SIMPSON

HOLLY GOES LIGHTLY

The X Factor presenter Holly Willoughby had a momentary lapse in a recent interview. Asked whether she thought Simon Cowell was a pop Svengali she responded in confusion: 'Is he from Svengali? I didn't know that. Is Svengali in Africa?'

'I may be a dumb blonde, but I'm not that blonde.'
PATRICIA NEAL

BLONDES ON THE MAP

In central parts of Norway, Sweden and Finland at least 80 per cent of the population is fair-haired. Away from this core area, fair hair becomes more of a rarity. The highest percentages of fair-haired people can be found around the Baltic Sea (Denmark, the Polish coast and the Baltic states). Icelanders share the same proportion of blondes as central Norway, while northern Britain, excluding the Highlands (full of dark-haired Celts), corresponds well with southern Norway at 50 to 79 per cent.

CAB, INNIT?

A nineteen-year-old Londoner called directory inquiries and asked for the number of a cab company to take her to Bristol airport. Instead of the word 'taxi', she used the Cockney rhyming slang: 'Joe Baxi'. When the operator couldn't find anyone of that name, the teen replied, 'It ain't a person, it's a cab, innit?' But the operator put the girl through to the nearest cabinet-makers. She then spoke to a bemused saleswoman and eventually sighed, 'Look, love, how hard is it? All I want is your cheapest cab, innit! I need it for ten in the morning. How much is it?' The sales advisor said it would be £180 and so the girl gave her address and paid with a credit card. Next morning an office cabinet was delivered to her home in South London.

The firm has now apologized for the mix-up and refunded her cash: 'We thought it was a joke at first but the girl was absolutely livid. We have suggested that maybe she should speak a bit more clearly on the phone.'

RICHARD, NOT JUDY

The acknowledged king and queen of daytime television Richard Madeley and Judy Finnegan are loved as much for their spontaneity and warmth as their programming style. In terms of blonde moments, though, it's really Richard who takes the lion's share.

Viewers watched helplessly as, during a general discussion about Viagra, Richard gave an appalling personal insight.

'We had one each,' he declared. 'It makes everything last much longer and return, you know, swiftly and hang around all day.' Other stunning examples of Richard's blondness abound, but here are some of the best, or rather worst (and we'll just cast a veil over the Ali G episode):

'I REALLY love ducks – they've always got a smile on their face.'

'You looked as if your head was going to come off!'
(AFTER WATCHING A CLIP OF A MAN SUFFERING FROM A STUTTER)

'How's your wife?'
(TO OPENLY GAY PET SHOP BOYS VOCALIST NEIL TENNANT)

'Do you think it's time we took a radical approach to dealing with paedophiles, as opposed to fiddling with the edges?'

'You're quite sharp. It's just that in the pure sense of the word, you're ignorant.'
(TO JADE GOODY)

'Where did you get your face? It's Egyptian, almost cat-like. What's it like without make-up?'
(TO SINGER SOPHIE ELLIS-BEXTOR)

'You're just humming with sexual energy! Is it
the fabric? Is it wearing tights?'
(TO TRANSVESTITE ARTIST GRAYSON PERRY)

NO JOKE IN HUNGARY

In 2004, blonde jokes were banned in Budapest after a group of angry women staged a demonstration outside parliament. The women handed in a petition that claimed they were being discriminated against in every walk of life by bad-taste blonde jokes.

Blondes – both natural and bleached – waved banners outside the ministry with slogans such as 'We're blonde, not stupid' and 'Love us for our minds'. Spokesperson Zsuzsa Kovacs said: 'Blondes face discrimination in the job market, in the workplace and even on the streets. People are banned from discriminating against Jews or black people, so why not grant blondes the same protection?'

HITCHCOCK'S BLONDES

'Hitchcock, with his blondes, captures all
my mystical feelings about women.'
CAMILLE PAGLIA

Master of suspense Alfred Hitchcock only cast blondes as
the leading ladies in his movies. He was truly obsessed
with a certain kind of blonde: ice-icons with an untouch-
able quality. In the late 1950s Columbia Pictures was
keen to find a new alternative to Marilyn Monroe and Rita
Hayworth, both of whom had become unpredictable, if
not downright flaky, and so peroxided Kim Novak landed
the lead as lonely Judy in *Vertigo*.

Though not Hitchcock's first choice, she went on to
produce the best performance of her career. Platinum hair
was intrinsic to the role because the hero (James Stewart as
Scottie) persuades her character to go blonde and to agree
to a makeover so that she looks more like Madeleine, his
supposedly lost love. The whole charade goes a stage
further when he persuades her to pin her
hair up in a certain way until finally she
metamorphoses into his ideal woman.

BLONDE IS THE NEW BLACK

Gianni Versace believed women liked being blonde. He described the state of blondeness as 'a triumph of femininity – like a cult'.

'Whoever said orange was the new pink was seriously disturbed.'
REESE WITHERSPOON (AS ELLE WOODS), *LEGALLY BLONDE*

'I think everybody should have a great Wonderbra. There's so many ways to enhance them – everybody does it.'
CHRISTINA AGUILLERA

'For me being blonde is not just having a hair colour; it is a way of being and a state of mind.'
DONATELLA VERSACE

'I don't do fashion, I am fashion.'
COCO CHANEL

WONDERWOMAN

Top model Eva Herzigova was an ash blonde, during her meteoric rise to fame. According to her, 'it's all about a moment in your life'. Eva became a household name with the 'Hello, Boys!' Wonderbra poster campaign. Later, when separated and quietly working her way round the world, she commented, 'At this moment I'm so much happier being dark.'

'All that tits and ass, the bullet bra, the cinched-in waist, the sewn-on dress. It all added up to the "Ooh, it's a blonde" sex factor.'
HAIR GURU ART LUNA ON HOLLYWOOD STYLE

'What's so great about going blonde is that with so little you can change yourself so much.'
TOP SESSION STYLIST ORLANDO PITA

SUPERBLONDES

'For models the moment they go blonde their
careers take off.'
GIANNI VERSACE

Of course, it's unfair to typecast supermodels as being
particularly prone to blonde moments. Take Linda Evangelista's infamous quote, referring to herself and fellow
supermodel Christy Turlington, 'We don't wake up for less
than $10,000 a day.' Now there's one astute blonde . . .
Here are some of her best moments:

'I don't diet. I just don't eat as much as
I'd like to.'

'I can do anything you want me to do, so long
as I don't have to speak.'

'It was God who made me so beautiful.
If I weren't, then I'd be a teacher.'

LINDA EVANGELISTA

KISS ME, KATE

In September 2007, supermodel Kate Moss was dropped by seven brands following what *The Sun* newspaper described as her 'cocaine honeymoon'. Then, to top it off, that summer her former boyfriend, singer Pete Doherty, was alleged to have cheated on her.

However, according to Forbes.com, Moss now earns more money than she did before her cocaine scandal and she is currently the second highest paid model in the world (next to Gisele Bündchen) as the face of Donna Karan, Yves Saint-Laurent and Roberto Cavalli for spring 2008.

She was set to marry her new boyfriend, guitarist Jamie Hince of The Kills, but the couple are in the middle of a cooling-off period. Doherty, meanwhile, is convinced he and Moss are star-crossed lovers and destined to be together.

Despite her undoubted ability to turn everything round, like other mere mortals Moss still has her blonde moments:

> 'Now I can walk into a room full of people I don't know and do my job. That's quite a massive thing to learn, I think.'

> 'People don't hear me talk. They don't
> expect me to.'
> KATE MOSS

Kate Moss was once introduced to presenter Jeremy Clarkson, who explained: 'I do *Top Gear*.' Kate looked puzzled, or so the story goes. 'What, are you a drug dealer or something?' she is alleged to have asked. Gentleman that he is, Clarkson denies this ever happened.

On the other hand, David Cameron, leader of the Tory party, claimed on ITV's *Parkinson* show that Ms Moss mistook him for a plumber. While this seems unlikely, many suspect that he'd be more than happy to nip round and check her pipes.

FASHION SENSE

●

> 'In the studio, I do try to have a thought in
> my head, so that it's not like a blank stare.'
> CINDY CRAWFORD

> 'I live my life day by day, and that's how
> I continue to live it.'
> NAOMI CAMPBELL

'I actually don't meet very many men because they are, I guess, afraid to approach me or think I'm from another planet.'

'I'm always amazed when I see mothers in high heels with kids. I'm like, how do you run after them?'

CLAUDIA SCHIFFER ON MEN AND CHILDREN

VIVE LA DIFFÉRENCE

As a thirteen-year-old, a blonde friend of the author was on an exchange visit to France and hoping to improve her French. She was enjoying dinner with her host family and some of their friends, and at the end of the meal, the mother of the French student asked my friend (in French) if she had had enough to eat. She replied, '*Je suis pleine*' (thinking this means 'I'm full'). What she actually said was, 'I'm pregnant.' Of course, this completely changed the atmosphere of the party.

RHYTHM AND BLONDES

'The hippies wanted peace and love. We wanted Ferraris, blondes and switchblades.'
ALICE COOPER

'I may not have the type of voice you like, but I can sing. You can't take that away from me, 'cos singing is a gift from God, and when people say I can't sing, it's kind of like insulting God.'
FERGIE, VOCALIST IN THE BLACK EYED PEAS

'Music is wonderful. Especially if there's some kind of content to it.'
DEBBIE HARRY

'Sometimes you have to sacrifice your performance for high heels.'
GWEN STEFANI

'My grandma was like, "Oh, Christina, you look like a whore!" I explained that's the idea.'
CHRISTINA AGUILLERA ON HER *MOULIN ROUGE* VIDEO FOR 'LADY MARMALADE'

'He [ex-husband Rod Stewart] was so mean it
hurt him to go to the bathroom.'
SWEDISH ACTRESS BRITT EKLAND

'I pick my nose and I'm not ashamed to admit
it. If there's a bogey then just pick it, man!'
JUSTIN TIMBERLAKE

'We sang a couple of duets in the car once.
They didn't go so well.'
CAMERON DIAZ (ON FORMER BOYFRIEND JUSTIN TIMBERLAKE)

'There's Elvis and me. I couldn't say
which of the two is best.'
LIAM GALLAGHER

BOTTOMS UP

In July 2002, waxworks museum Madame Tussauds unveiled a new tribute to iconic princess of pop Kylie Minogue in a provocative all-fours pose. Later, it was reported that the museum had lengthened the skirt on what had become its most popular model. Although the allegation was denied, a spokeswoman for the museum offered the following qualification: 'The skirt may appear shorter in some pictures because photographers have been a bit naughty and have been pushing it up to get a good picture of her bottom.'

Songs for blondes
'White on Blonde' - Texas
'Whiter Shade of Pale' - Procol Harum
'Dirty Blonde' - Courtney Love
'Blonde on Blonde' - Bob Dylan
'Suicide Blonde' - INXS
'Heart of Glass' - Blondie
'White Wedding' - Billy Idol
'Blondes in Black Cars' - Autograph

SAY WHAT?!

'Osama bin Laden is the only one who knows
what I'm going through.'
SINGER R. KELLY ON HIS ARREST FOLLOWING ACCUSATIONS OF
TWENTY-ONE COUNTS OF HAVING SEX WITH A MINOR IN 2002

'My child was not only carried by me,
but by the universe.'
CELINE DION

'I'm an ocean because I'm really deep.
If you search deep you can find rare
exotic treasures.'
CHRISTINA AGUILLERA

AMY WINEHOUSE HAS A
BLONDE MOMENT

Amid charges of assault and conspiracy, Amy Winehouse's
husband, Blake Fielder-Civil, was led away from court in
January 2008. Renowned for her black beehive, the newly
platinum – if somewhat bedraggled – Amy blew kisses,

yelling out, 'I love you, handsome gorgeous one,' before adding to reporters, 'I am not talking to you!'

'I have tried sex with both men and women.
I found I liked it.'
DUSTY SPRINGFIELD

MADGE

A teacher remembers being surrounded by a horde of Bath prep schoolboys back at the beginning of the eighties. 'Sir, sir, do you like Madonna, sir?' Out of touch even then, he asked advice of the (blond) class swot. 'What do you think, Simpson?' Looking up from his Latin dictionary with a sigh, the nine-year-old replied, 'Just another clever Italian-American on the make, sir.'

'Everyone probably thinks that I'm a raving nymphomanic, that I have an insatiable sexual appetite, when the truth is, I'd rather read a book.'
(MADONNA RECENTLY REVEALED THAT SHE AND HER HUSBAND SLEEP WITH THEIR BLACKBERRYS.)

'I am certainly not against plastic surgery. However, I am absolutely against having to discuss it.'

'Dress like Britney Spears and think like me, and everything will be fine.'

MADONNA

BLONDE JOKES #2

A blonde finds a genie's lamp and so she rubs it. A genie pops out and says that she can have three wishes, but all the other blondes in the world will have double the number of wishes. So she says that she wants a mansion. The genie says OK, but all the other blondes in the world will get *two* mansions. On her next wish she asks for two boyfriends. So the genie says that all the other blondes in the world will get *four* boyfriends. On her last wish she says, 'You see that baseball bat over there, I want you to beat me *half* to death with it!'

✳

A blonde called Sharon finds herself in dire straits: her business has gone bust. She decides to pray for help: 'God, please help me! I've lost my business and I'm going to lose my house as well. Please let me win the lottery.' Lottery night comes and someone else wins. Sharon again prays, 'God, please let me win the lottery! I've lost my house, my business and I'm going to lose my car as well.' But lottery night comes round and still she doesn't win. Once more she prays, 'My God, why have you forsaken me? I've lost my business, my house and my car. My kids are starving! I don't often ask you for help. *Please* let me win the lottery just this once so I can get my life in order.' Suddenly there's a blinding flash of light as the heavens open. Sharon hears the voice of God himself: 'Sharon, meet me halfway on this – *buy a ticket*!'

✳

Two blondes walk into a building. Surely one of them must have seen it.

✳

At a party a blonde tells her friend that she's gone off men: 'They lie, they cheat and they're just no good,' she complains. 'From now on when I want sex, I'm going to use my tried and tested plastic companion.' Her friend asks: 'What happens when your batteries run out?' She replies: 'Easy: I'll just fake an orgasm, as usual.'

FOOTBALLERS' WIVES

There's a certain look that's synonymous with WAGs: blonde hair (natural or enhanced), fake tan, lots of bling and designer clothes, especially handbags. But this form of blondeness is not restricted to physical appearance – as has already been proven, blonde moments can affect anyone, regardless of hair colour or style, and some WAGs break the mould altogether. Let's start with Victoria Beckham:

'I haven't read a book in my life.'

'I don't know much about football. I know what a goal is, which is surely the main thing about football.'

'I am not going to be no senorita.'

'A lot of the houses I looked at were really garish – lots of gold, all very Versace. David and I do have good taste. I like everything to be simple and plain.'
(ON THE BECKHAMS' MOVE TO SPAIN)

'Let me tell you what the real David Beckham is addicted to - *Extreme Makeover*. He sits in bed watching that and loves Alan Tichmarsh in *Ground Force* - that's what he's really like.'

'David is very tidy - even our fridge is colour-coded. He vacuums in straight lines, even in a pinny. If anyone walks around after he's done it, he gets funny.'

<small>VICTORIA BECKHAM</small>

LILY V. CHERYL

'A chick with a dick.'
GIRLS ALOUD WAG CHERYL COLE'S DESCRIPTION OF
SINGER-SONGWRITER LILY ALLEN

'Taking your clothes off, doing sexy dancing and marrying a rich footballer must be very gratifying; your mother must be so proud.'
LILY ALLEN'S RESPONSE

EXTENDED TRAVELS

There were suggestions that Coleen McLoughlin may have left the World Cup in Germany in 2006 to travel 1400 miles back to Liverpool for hair extensions. Her publicists refused to confirm or deny the story. Despite some negativity from the press, the new Mrs Rooney has her own magazine column, a best-selling book, a fragrance, a fitness DVD and now her own TV series, *Coleen's Real Women*.

THE SHARPER SIDE OF BLONDE

'Just standing around looking beautiful is
so boring, really boring, so boring.'
MICHELLE PFEIFFER

'My mother said it was simple to keep a man:
you must be a maid in the living room, a cook
in the kitchen and a whore in the bedroom.
I said I'd hire the other two and take care
of the bedroom bit!'
JERRY HALL

'He was telling me he doesn't think he'll get
into heaven . . . I'm thinking, "If you're not
going to heaven, then I am screwed!"'
CHARLIZE THERON ON MEETING NELSON MANDELA

'I'm not offended by dumb blonde jokes
because I know I'm not dumb . . . I also know
I'm not blonde!'
DOLLY PARTON

'Women might be able to fake orgasms but men
can fake whole relationships.'
SHARON STONE

'Every man I meet wants to protect me.
I can't figure out what from.'
MAE WEST

'I ask people why they have deer heads on
their walls. They always say it's because
it's such a beautiful animal. There you go.
I think my mother is attractive but
I have photographs of her.'
ELLEN DEGENERES

'She [Patsy] was so anally retentive
she couldn't sit down for fear of
sucking up the furniture.'
JOANNA LUMLEY ON HER CHARACTER, CHAIN-SMOKING PR DIVA
PATSY, IN *ABSOLUTELY FABULOUS*

STEEL MAGNOLIA

In a bitter courtroom battle, £500-an-hour legal ace Fiona Shackleton saved her client, Sir Paul McCartney, just over £100 million in his divorce from ex-model (and fellow blonde) Heather Mills. Ms Shackleton (christened 'Steel Magnolia' by colleagues) entered the court on 17 March 2008 immaculately coiffed in her usual bouffant style, only to leave looking a little dampened but not discomfited when Mills threw a glass of water over her head following the £24.3 million settlement.

In fact, 'Splashgate' may have been a blessing in disguise, for Shackleton had inadvertently been given a makeover that was sleek, smooth and slightly sexy in place of her regular style, which seemed glued together with gallons of hairspray. Men, women and fashion journalists everywhere applauded her.

'Don't you know that a man being rich is like a girl being pretty? You wouldn't marry a girl just because she's pretty, but my goodness, doesn't it help?'
MARILYN MONROE AS LORELEI LEE IN
GENTLEMEN PREFER BLONDES

BLONDE TECHNOLOGY

BLONDE VIRUS WARNING!

You have just received the 'Blonde Virus'!
Since we don't have any programming experience, this virus works on the honesty system. Please delete all the files on your hard drive then manually forward this virus to everyone on your mailing list.

OK

Q: How do you know when a blonde's been using your computer?
A: There's cheese in front of the mouse.

Q: How do you tell if another blonde's been using your computer?
A: There's Tippex on the screen.

Q: And if a third blonde's been using your computer?
A: There's writing on the Tippex.

A blonde calls the IT help desk with a printing problem. The technician asks if she's running it under Windows, to which the woman responds, 'No, my desk is next to the door. But that's a good point. There's a man sitting opposite me under a window and his machine is working fine.'

TALL STORY

Producer David O. Selznick often poured his concerns into his famous memos. In one such note, addressed to Kay Brown in the story department, he talks of Swedish bombshell Ingrid Bergman, whom he had already cast in *Intermezzo* in 1939: 'I note Bergman is five feet, nine and a half inches tall. Is it possible that she is actually this high and do you think we will have to use step-ladders for Leslie Howard?'

'There's a sculpture in our bedroom, a solid brass replica of Antonio's manhood. It's very expensive. He gave it to me as a romantic gift.'
MELANIE GRIFFITH

BLONDE MAGIC

The American television series *Bewitched* was first broadcast in 1964 and ran for eight series until 1972. In it, Elizabeth Montgomery plays Samantha Stephens, a beautiful young blonde, who is also a powerful member of a society of witches that has lived apart from human society for many centuries. She falls in love with a young advertising executive, Darrin Stephens, and, to the disgust of her family, she vows to give up witchcraft altogether.

On her honeymoon, she tells her new husband that she is a witch with magic powers, but she promises that she will only use her magic to help Darrin and herself. Throughout the series, Samantha's relatives invade their household and use magic to drive her husband crazy.

Bewitched marked the first time that a married couple, played by unmarried actors, was seen in the same bed together on TV. Before this, most shows featured married couples in separate beds.

STAGE AND SCREEN

Although Doris Day is said to have got along with most of her co-stars on *Calamity Jane*, one exception was Martha Hyer, who played her love rival. On Doris's request, naturally blonde Martha was forced to dye her hair brunette – or leave the production.

'The more flesh you show, the higher up the ladder you go.'
JERRY HALL

THEM'S THE RULES . . .

Jane Fonda was once a student at Vassar, then strictly a women's college. In those days, the standard attire for afternoon tea was a pair of elegant white gloves and a string of pearls. When confronted with the issue, she obediently returned to her room and thence to the parlour wearing the requisite gloves and pearls . . . and nothing else.

'If you obey all the rules, you miss all the fun.'
KATHARINE HEPBURN

BIT OF A BOOB . . . OR PERHAPS A CAREER MOVE?

Famously well-endowed blonde actress Jayne Mansfield, whose studio chair simply stated '40-21-35', somehow managed to 'accidentally' upstage her fellow actresses with her amazing breasts.

During a publicity shoot for Jane Russell's movie *Underwater*, Mansfield fell into the water. Sure enough, her swimsuit strap popped off and she resurfaced topless.

SAUCY

At an Oscars ceremony Helen Mirren was asked if she had a 'naughty streak' to which she replied, 'No, I am good through and through – I'm an Essex girl.'

MOVIE-STAR QUOTES

'I think that *Clueless* was very deep. I think
it was deep in the way that it was very light.
I think lightness has to come from a very
deep place if it's true lightness.'
ALICIA SILVERSTONE

'If someone were to harm my family or a
friend or somebody I love, I would eat them.
I might end up in jail for five hundred
years, but I would eat them.'
JOHNNY DEPP

'Once I put that wig on, I didn't say an
intelligent thing for four months.
My voice went up. I walked differently.
I'd ask incredibly stupid questions.'
SIGOURNEY WEAVER ON THE BLONDE WIG SHE SPORTED FOR
THE FILM *GALAXY QUEST*

'I will have one of the cleanest obits of
any actress. I never did cheesecake like Ann
Sheridan or Betty Grable. I just used my hair.'
VERONICA LAKE

'I say I don't sleep with married men, but what I mean is that I don't sleep with *happily* married men.'
SWEDISH ACTRESS BRITT EKLAND

'I'm really over looking at people squeezed into their jeans. I don't want to know that much about anybody!'
UMA THURMAN

MARILYN MONROE

'There was my name in lights. I said, "God, somebody's made a mistake!" But there it was, in lights. And I sat there and said, "Remember, you're not a star." Yet there it was in lights.'

'I knew I belonged to the public and to the world, not because I was talented or even beautiful, but because I had never belonged to anything or anyone else.'

'Arthur Miller wouldn't have married me if I had been nothing but a dumb blonde.'

Facts about Marilyn

* In 1999 she was named *Playboy* magazine's Number One Sex Star of the Twentieth Century.

* She was crowned Miss California Artichoke Queen in 1947.

* Her studio claimed her measurements were 37-23-36, while her dressmaker reported that she was actually 35-22-35.

* She starred in thirty movies, including *Some Like It Hot* (1960) and *The Prince and the Showgirl* (1959).

* 'Lemon Marilyn', Andy Warhol's silkscreen work, was sold for $250 not long after her death in 1962. In 2007 it was up for auction at Christie's and sold for more than $28 million.

* On 29 June 1956 she married the playwright Arthur Miller in a Jewish ceremony.

* Her last public appearance was on 1 June 1962.

* She died in her Brentwood, California home on 5 August 1962.

* The songs 'Happy Birthday, Mr President', 'Diamonds Are a Girl's Best Friend' and 'I Wanna Be Loved by You' will be forever associated with her.

THE 'OTHER' PLATINUM BLONDE

Screen legend Jean Harlow (1911–37) eloped at the age of sixteen. In 1930 she purred her most famous line, 'Excuse me while I slip into something more comfortable' in the classic film *Hell's Angels*. The following year, she won the starring role in the suitably titled *Platinum Blonde*. Her other films include *Bombshell*, *Goldie* and *Reckless*.

'There are only three ages for women in Hollywood: *Babe*, *District Attorney* and *Driving Miss Daisy*.'
GOLDIE HAWN

PLAIN AND PROUD

'I don't judge others. I say if you feel good with what you're doing, let your freak flag fly.'

In October 2007 Sarah Jessica Parker of *Sex and the City* fame was given the dubious honour of being named 'Unsexiest Woman Alive' in an online poll by men's website Maxim.com. While women love her effortless quirky style, it seems many men just don't get it. SJP later admitted she was devastated at being awarded the unflattering title and couldn't bring herself to tell her husband, Matthew Broderick. She commented, 'It's so brutal in a way, so filled with rage and anger. But, on the other hand, I really like the choices I've made. I am who I am.'

SCARLETT JOHANSSON ON LIFE AND LOVE

'I like my body and face, and I love my breasts . . . my girls.'

'I've never considered myself a femme fatale as I've never seduced anyone and ruined their lives – at least as far as I know.'

'Maybe I had one too many champagne cocktails but I got home and opened up my door and it wasn't my kitchen! I realized my key opens up somebody else's door in my building!'

AN AUDIENCE WITH CAMERON DIAZ

'I can spend hours in a grocery store; I get so excited when I see food, I go crazy. I spend hours arranging my basket so that everything fits in and nothing gets squashed. I'm really anal about it, actually.'

'I've been noticing gravity since I was very young.'

'I'm not ashamed of being a bubbly, funny person. I think that's as valid as being the dark, brooding, tortured Oscar-nominated one.'

'I'd kiss a frog even if there was no promise of a Prince Charming popping out of it. I love frogs.'

I'M A BLONDE!

Former squeeze of rocker Marilyn Manson, burlesque star Dita Von Teese is really a natural blonde. Recently, she revealed that her famous jet-black locks are the result of constant treatments over the past sixteen years. The porcelain-skinned beauty admits that she disliked her naturally fair hair when she was younger and experimented with different colours until she settled on black. But she insists her raven hair was not picked to match the gothic style of her ex-husband. The 34-year-old star said, 'I have been dyeing my hair since I was eighteen. First I was platinum blonde, then red, then burgundy. Finally, one day there was nowhere else to go but black. I like the contrast between pale skin and dark hair.'

'I think any girl who comes to Hollywood with "sex symbol" or "bombshell" hanging over her has a rough road'
KIM BASINGER

JOAN RIVERS V. MISS GREAT BRITAIN

The ever-charming Joan Rivers drew criticism for her acidic comments as compère for Miss Great Britain 2007. As contenders from all corners of Great Britain (and Northern Ireland, confusingly) vied for the judges' attention and insisted there was no sexism in the contest, Rivers made some of the choicest asides of the evening:

'My advice to these girls? Marry rich immediately – immediately – so everything is in place. If you can meet someone tonight, leave the contest in the centre of it, you dumb bitch.'

'Everyone thinks all these girls have great bodies but are stupid. That's not true. There are fifty of them, and two are really nice and smart; they knew their names. The rest, well ... I shouted, "Hey tramp!" backstage and they turned around and said, "Yes?"'

MORE GEMS FROM JOAN . . .

'Before we make love, my husband takes
a painkiller.'

'Boy George is all England needs – another
queen who can't dress.'

'I wish I had a twin so I could know what
I'd look like without plastic surgery.'

THE *BAYWATCH* BABE

Model, movie star, worldwide sex symbol and animal rights campaigner Pamela Anderson recently admitted her most embarrassing moment was 'not realizing that Ugg boots were made from sheepskin.' When asked what she disliked most about her appearance, The *Baywatch* star quipped drily: 'Being bald – I wish I didn't have to wear these big blonde wigs every day' and also that 'any drag queen' would do to play her in the film of her life.

Three times married but single once more, she said the most important lesson that life had taught her was that 'Opportunity only gives you the knockers once.' Her modelling career began when she was filmed at a football game wearing a Labatt T-shirt, prompting the beer company to hand her a modelling contract. Here's a showcase of some of her best blonde moments:

'It's great being blonde. With such low expectations, it's easy to impress.'

'I've been fortunate: I haven't had too many auditions. I slept with the right people.'

'I have to meet someone who loves children and who loves ex-husbands and implants.'

'I wanted to retire from all that, but I guess my breasts still have a career and I'm just tagging along with them.'

'I've always had good penis karma. I used to say I had never seen a small one but recently maybe I have.'

'Beyond its entertainment value, *Baywatch* has enriched and, in so many cases, helped save lives.'
DAVID HASSELHOFF

GENTLEMEN PREFER BLONDES

The 1953 movie featured Marilyn Monroe's iconic rendition of 'Diamonds Are a Girl's Best Friend'. Dripping with jewels, she struts her stuff as money-mad Lorelei Lee in a pink satin number with matching gloves, surrounded by adoring men, who offer her still more jewels. Dark-haired Jane Russell plays Dorothy Shaw, Lorelei's best friend.

Despite director Howard Hawks' approval of takes, Monroe insisted on retakes. When Twentieth Century Fox asked how production might be speeded up, Hawks retorted: 'Three wonderful ideas: replace Marilyn, rewrite the script and make it shorter, and get a new director!'

It was to be Russell's only film with Monroe, but the blonde and brunette got on so well that Russell was often the only person who could coax Marilyn out of her trailer to begin the day's filming and she fondly christened her 'Blondie'.

'It is possible that blondes also prefer gentlemen.'
MAMIE VAN DOREN, VARGA GIRL AND ACTRESS

Sienna Miller: 'I just wanted to say I
can't believe I'm sitting in
a bar, drinking champagne
next to Kevin Bacon.'

Kevin Spacey: 'Spacey.'

Sienna: 'Yeah, it is, isn't it?'

TEN GREAT BLONDE ACTRESSES

* Grace Kelly
* Marilyn Monroe
* Jean Harlow
* Tippy Hendron
* Veronica Lake
* Brigitte Bardot
* Gwyneth Paltrow
* Sissy Spacek
* Charlize Theron
* Meryl Streep

BLONDE MOMENTS FROM *BRIDGET JONES*

Interviewer: 'What do you think about the El Nino phenomenon?'

Bridget: 'It's a blip – Latin music's on its way out.'

*

Bridget answers the phone: 'Bridget Jones, wanton sex goddess with a very bad man between her thighs . . . Mum! Hi!'

*

TV producer: 'Why do you wanna work in television?'

Bridget: 'I've got to leave my job because I shagged my boss.'

TV producer: 'Fair enough. Start on Monday.'

PARIS HILTON'S HIGHLIGHTS

'[Kabbalah] helps you confront your fears. Like, if a girl borrowed my clothes and never gave them back, and I saw her wearing them months later, I would confront her.'

'If I could read a book, I'd definitely read one of yours.'
(To NOVELIST JACKIE COLLINS)

'Nicky [Paris's sister] and I are different in this crucial way: she's better at shopping than I am.'

'Wal-mart . . . do they make walls there?'

'Whenever I write an e-mail, it doesn't mean anything – it's just words I write.'

'One time I arrived at a party in a helicopter. I kind of felt bad because the wind from the propellers blew champagne glasses out of people's hands. But I thought it was cool.'

'I'll pick out two outfits, one which is disgusting and one nice, and I'll ask my "friend" what they think. If they go for the revolting one, I cut them out of my life.'
(ON TIDYING UP HER ADDRESS BOOK)

'Every decade has an iconic blonde like Marilyn Monroe or Princess Diana, and right now, I'm that icon.'

BLONDE MEANS . . .

* putting custard through a sieve to remove the lumps
  . . . but doing it over the sink

* dropping something (expensive) in the loo, flushing
  to clean it off . . . and losing it

* putting the iron in the fridge (but only when
  you're *really* tired)

* draining potatoes through a plastic sieve, but then
  putting it in the oven to keep warm, only to produce
  molten wax

* marking your opponent on the hockey pitch . . .
  even when she goes off to get a tissue

* leaving the bedroom window open so the breeze
  causes a mirror to fall down in the bathroom, causing
  an almighty crash, then freaking out and calling the
  emergency services when you think it's a burglar.

(These are all real moments etched forever into the
memories of some of the author's blonder girlfriends.)

BLONDE JOKES #3

A blonde and a redhead meet in a bar in New York after work and are watching the six o'clock news. A man is threatening to jump from Brooklyn Bridge. The blonde bets the redhead $50 he won't jump and the redhead replies, 'I'll take that bet!' Unfortunately, the man jumps and so the blonde gives her friend the $50. 'I can't take this, you're my friend,' says the redhead. But the blonde insists, 'No, a bet's a bet.' 'Listen, I have to admit I saw this on the five o'clock news, so I can't take your money,' says the redhead. Silence . . . and then the blonde says, 'Well, so did I. But I never thought he'd jump again.'

*

A businessman enters an elevator. Inside is a blonde, who greets him by saying, 'T.G.I.F.' He smiles at her, but replies, 'S.H.I.T.' Puzzled, she repeats, 'T.G.I.F.' Again, he acknowledges her remark with 'S.H.I.T.' A little hurt, the blonde still manages to smile her biggest smile and says as sweetly as possible, 'T.G.I.F.' another time. This time the man smiles back at her, but once again he replies, 'S.H.I.T.' Finally, the blonde decides to explain things, 'T.G.I.F: Thank Goodness It's Friday – get it?' 'Sorry, honey, it's Thursday,' he replies.

*

Three blondes are stranded on an island. They discover a lamp, rub it and out pops a genie who says, 'I'll grant each of you a wish.' The first blonde wished to be more intelligent than the other two; she goes bald and swims off the island. The second blonde wanted to be more intelligent than the other two; she turns into a redhead, builds a raft and rows off the island. Finally, the last blonde asked to be more intelligent than the other two . . . she turns into a brunette and walks across the bridge.

*

Q: Why do blondes leave empty milk cartons in the fridge?
A: In case anyone wants black coffee!

Playboy founder Hugh Hefner was once asked whether blondes really have more fun. 'They do with me!' he replied.

WHAT'S COOKING?

'I never worry about diets. The only carrots that interest me are the number you get in a diamond.'
MAE WEST

Try these scrumptiously sweet blondes with a difference:

Butterscotch Blondies
Makes 36

*175g butter, softened,
plus extra for greasing
175g light brown sugar
115g granulated sugar
2 eggs
230g plain flour
1 tsp bicarbonate of soda
½ tsp salt
300g butterscotch chips
150g chopped nuts*

1. Preheat the oven to 140°C/275°F/Gas mark 1. Meanwhile, grease a deep baking tray.

2. In a large bowl, beat together the butter, brown sugar and granulated sugar until light and creamy. Add the eggs, beating well.

3. Stir together the flour, bicarbonate of soda and salt. Gradually add to the creamed butter mixture, beating until well blended.

4. Stir in the butterscotch chips and nuts, if using. Spread the mixture evenly over the surface of the greased tray using a palette knife. Bake for 30–35 minutes or until the top is golden brown and the centre is set.

5. Cool completely in the tray then slice into bars.

Perfect for an afternoon snack attack!

'The best thing I have is the knife from *Fatal Attraction*. I hung it in my kitchen. It's my way of saying, "Don't mess with me!"'
GLENN CLOSE, ACTRESS (AND FORMER BUNNY-BOILER)

BLONDE CULINARY QUOTES

'French fries; I love them. Some people are chocolate-and-sweets people. I love French fries - that, and caviar.'
CAMERON DIAZ

'If I've learned nothing else, it's that if you keep on shouting at the top of your voice, in the end you just piss people off.'
JAMIE OLIVER

'She [Joan Collins] thought that the price of the meal would be on the house. I told her the only thing on the house was the roof!'
GORDON RAMSAY

SCOOTER SKILLS

In May 2003 'Naked Chef' Jamie Oliver made a memorable appearance on *The Oprah Winfrey Show*. The producers came up with the great idea of having him enter the set on his trademark scooter and Oliver was only too happy to oblige.

'The thing was, the floor was really polished and the tyres were brand new. Before I knew it, I stacked it, flew about a metre in the air and landed on my chest. I had a really silky bodywarmer on and I slid about three and half metres, with my arms in some sort of superman pose, using my chin as a brake,' he later recalled. 'I think it was the funniest thing that has ever happened to me but I felt a complete idiot. The audience loved it – I think they thought I did it on purpose. I jumped up and they gave me a cheer.'

A blonde goes to the doctor's with scalded feet. 'How did that happen?' asks the doctor. 'Cooking soup,' she replies. 'The instructions said: "Open can, stand in boiling water for seven minutes."'

COCKTAIL HOUR

'I was in love with a beautiful blonde once,
dear. She drove me to drink. It's the one thing
I am indebted to her for.'
W. C. FIELDS, *NEVER GIVE A SUCKER AN EVEN BREAK* (1941)

Parisian Blonde

25 ml double cream
a little caster sugar
25 ml orange curaçao
25 ml dark rum
crushed ice
orange slices, to decorate

Place all the ingredients in a cocktail shaker and shake
well. Strain into a cocktail glass and decorate with orange
slices.

Cosmopolitan

The drink enjoyed by the blonde that almost every girl would love to have as her best friend: Carrie Bradshaw, fictional newspaper columnist of *Sex and the City*.

50ml raspberry vodka
35ml Cointreau
juice of half a lime
75ml cranberry juice
2 strawberries, hulled,
plus one strawberry slice, to garnish
crushed ice
sugar, to garnish
strips of orange zest

Put all the ingredients into a shaker. Muddle in 2 strawberries, add crushed ice and shake vigorously. Strain into a tall martini glass rimmed with sugar, zest with orange peel and garnish with a slice of strawberry.

Beach Blonde

Ursula Andress was the first Bond blonde in 1962's *Dr No* and became a world-famous icon when she stalked the beach searching for conch in her role as Honey Ryder.

'Are you looking for shells?' she asked Bond.
'No,' he replied, 'I'm just looking . . .'

15 ml shot dark rum
50 ml advocaat
50 ml orange juice
half a banana
crushed ice

Blend all the ingredients together and serve in a highball glass.

Mae West

'You ought to get out of those wet clothes . . .
and into a dry martini.'
MAE WEST

The following drink was specially created for her.

> 90ml brandy
> 1 tsp caster sugar
> 1 egg yolk
> crushed ice
> cayenne pepper

Shake the brandy, sugar and egg yolk with the ice, then strain into a chilled cocktail glass. Lightly sprinkle with cayenne pepper and serve.

Golden Girl Cocktail

In honour of historic blondes everywhere . . . and also one of the best TV series of all time!

50ml gin
25ml sherry
dash each of orange bitters
and Angostura bitters

Stir the ingredients in a mixing glass with ice and then strain into a cocktail glass. Enjoy with a piece of cheesecake just like Dorothy, Blanche, Rose and Sofia.

COMMONS BLONDES

'Too full of drugs, obesity, underachievement and Labour MPs.'
BORIS JOHNSON ON PORTSMOUTH

'Oh, he just loves the sound of his own voice.'
CHERIE BLAIR (AFTER HER HUSBAND WAS THANKED BY A CLERGYMAN FOR DOING A READING AT A SERVICE IN BARBADOS)

'Well, he would, wouldn't he?'
MANDY RICE-DAVIS'S RESPONSE TO LORD ASTOR'S DENIALS THAT HE EVER MET HER — AND THE START OF THE SIXTIES PROFUMO SCANDAL. (THE INFAMOUS BLONDE WENT ON TO DABBLE IN ACTING, WROTE A NUMBER OF NOVELS AND EVENTUALLY MARRIED A MILLIONAIRE.)

THE LADY'S NOT FOR TURNING

Following her election to the British Conservative Party Leadership in 1975, Margaret Thatcher made the decision to greet her cheering supporters with a Churchill 'V' sign. Unfortunately her fingers were the wrong way round when she delivered it!

'I am a conviction politician, like her.'
GORDON BROWN COMPARES HIMSELF TO MAGGIE

HILLARY RODHAM CLINTON

'If I want to knock a story off the front page, I just change my hairstyle.'

'We have a lot of kids who don't know what work means. They think work is a four-letter word.'

'If I didn't kick his ass every day, he [Bill Clinton] wouldn't be worth anything.'

'I have said that I'm not running and I'm
having a great time being Pres ... being
a first-term senator.'
(ON HER PRESIDENTIAL AMBITIONS)

'I'm not going to have some reporters pawing
through our papers. We are the President.'

And now it's Bill Clinton's turn:

'When I was in England, I experimented with
marijuana a time or two, and I didn't like it.
I didn't inhale and never tried it again.'

'You know, if I were a single man, I might ask
that mummy out. That's a good-looking mummy.'
(LOOKING AT 'JUANITA', AN INCAN MUMMY ON
DISPLAY AT THE NATIONAL GEOGRAPHIC MUSEUM)

'I'm someone who had a deep emotional
attachment to *Starsky and Hutch*.'

'Well, I don't have much job security.'
(WHEN ASKED IN 1992 WHY HE STILL PLAYED THE SAXOPHONE)

'I may not have been the greatest president
but I've had the most fun eight years.'

HAPPY BIRTHDAY, MR PRESIDENT

When Marilyn Monroe sang her birthday tribute to John F. Kennedy on 19 May 1962 at Madison Square Garden her dress was a sheer nylon slip with 2500 rhinestones sewn on to it. It was so snug she had to be sewn into it. She was also wearing a wig, which looked a little 'windswept', and it was rumoured that she had had sex with someone backstage just fifteen minutes before stepping onto the stage, although this was never proven.

Peter Lawford mocked her notorious lateness by giving her a really long introduction, during which she was supposed to come onstage several times. In the middle of his last attempt she sauntered on as he introduced her as 'the late Marilyn Monroe'. Following the legendary performance, JFK thanked her, saying, 'Now I can retire from politics after having had "Happy Birthday" sung to me in such a sweet, wholesome way.'

'If you ask me, I'd like to become the first female president. That would be really cool ... The first thing I would do is redecorate [the White House]. It doesn't look very cosy.'
JENNIFER LOPEZ'S GEOPOLITICAL STRATEGY

THE NEW DORIS DAY

MP Ann Widdecombe decided to go blonde after a House of Commons sketchwriter compared her locks to a zebra crossing. She admits men talk to her much more slowly these days. A popular figure in the Tory camp, admiring taxi drivers often toot their horns at her.

On one occasion, Widdecombe took a cab to a rally, armed with a pamphlet she had written on religion and ready to give her all. Unfortunately, once she stepped out, the taxi driver drove off with all the pamphlets still in the back. Undaunted, Widdecombe set off in hot pursuit, shouting into her megaphone: 'Stop, stop! I have lost my Christian principles.'

BROWN IS THE NEW BLONDE

More often than not, the beleaguered British PM is accused of being too dour and serious. However, he was left looking foolish after recklessly name-dropping music band The Arctic Monkeys in *New Woman* magazine, only to be caught out later when he was unable to name a single track on their new album and could only insist that they were 'very loud'. In fact, Brown's taste would seem to lean a little more towards 'disco' – he is known to be a good friend and fan of Robin Gibb of Bee Gees fame.

LONDON'S UNLIKELY LORD MAYOR

'Everybody in Cameron's office is crossing their fingers. Ken Livingstone knew about running a local authority –
Boris knows nothing.'
DIANE ABBOTT, LABOUR MP

A scene on the outskirts of Henley: Boris Johnson out campaigning to become the next Mayor of London. He enters a small enclave of council houses. Charlie Spires (a man with enormous white sideburns) stands on a ladder, cleaning his caravan with a toothbrush.

Boris (brightly): You're cleaning your caravan with a toothbrush! [Mr Spires eyes Boris as if he's wandered over from another planet.]

Boris (still brightly): Will you be voting Conservative?

Mr Spires: No way, Jacko!

Boris (undeterred): Right-ho, jolly good. Carry on toothbrushing!

Yet on 3 May 2008 the blond bombshell won the race to become Mayor of London. His colourful campaign trail included a spot of singing – 'Is This the Way to Amarillo' was perhaps a particular favourite of his. Despite (or because of) this, he brought Ken Livingstone's eight-year reign at City Hall to an end with 1,168,738 first and second preference votes, compared to Mr Livingstone's 1,028,966. The turnout was a record 45 per cent. 'I will work flat out to repay and to justify your confidence,' promised Boris, who was photographed three weeks later sporting a lurid pair of shorts on holiday with his family in Turkey.

'The Tory Party – the funkiest, most jiving Party on Earth!'

'My chances of being PM are about as good as the chances of finding Elvis on Mars, or my being reincarnated as an olive.'

'My friends, as I have discovered myself,
there are no disasters, only opportunities.
And, indeed, opportunities for disasters.'

'Voting Tory will cause your wife to have
bigger breasts and increase your chances
of owning a BMW M3.'

'What's my view on drugs?
I've forgotten my view on drugs.'
(DURING THE CAMPAIGN FOR THE 2005 GENERAL ELECTION)

'I love tennis with a passion. I challenged
Boris Becker to a match once and he said he
was up for it but he never called back.
I bet I could make him run around.'

BOMBER BORIS

In 2006 Boris Johnson took part in a charity football match. It was a light-hearted attempt to recreate the England v. Germany match of 1966. As the crowd chanted, 'We want Boris,' he limbered up, waving his arms about like a rusty helicopter. Their cheers grew and the chant 'Boris, Boris' became irresistible. With eight minutes to go, he passed (to a German). Then, in a fashion more suited to Twickenham, he launched himself at the oppostition's number six, Maurizio Gaudino. There was a roar from the crowd as the then MP for Henley powered his head into his stunned opponent's groin. Following the final whistle, Boris, lager in hand, said: 'There was no malice in my actions. I was going for the ball with my head, which I understand is a legitimate move . . . I felt an enormous sense of achievement every time I actually touched the ball.'

CONFUSED NEWS

One of the earliest known 'blonde moments' on radio was experienced by 1930s radio broadcaster Harry Von Zell, who became tongue-tied and introduced US President Herbert Hoover as 'Hoobert Heever'.

*

Recently, the usually cool and measured tones of Radio 4 newsreader Charlotte Green were broken by gales of laughter following a clip of the earliest known voice recording. Green was overtaken by a fit of the giggles after listening to a crackly voice singing 'Au Clair de la Lune' and corpsed all the way through the subsequent serious report on the death of a film producer. Green was voted radio's most-liked female voice but, on this occasion, the BBC switchboard was jammed with listener complaints. Fellow newsreaders came out in support and sympathy. Natasha Kaplinsky's solution when stifling laughter on air? 'I think "P45, P45."'

*

Former Sky News presenter Julie Etchingham, the first female anchor to cover election night in the UK, got into hot water with bosses and the Conservative party last year when she unwittingly made a political aside while on air. She was covering David Cameron's first major speech about Conservative policies on immigration. Cameron is heard to say, 'Let me outline the action that a Conservative government would take. As we have seen, some of the increase in population size results from natural change – birth rates, death rates. Here, our policy should be obvious . . .' At which point Etchingham interjects: 'Extermination', thinking her microphone was switched off. A senior source at the broadcaster dismissed it as a bit of a blonde moment: 'She was just being silly. It did not have any great import. As far as I can tell the Tories have accepted our apology.'

*

CNN is relatively relaxed compared to BBC news, nevertheless there were blushes all round in 2006 after anchor Kyra Phillips forgot to switch her microphone off during a trip to the ladies'. While George Bush continued a speech on Hurricane Katrina, Phillips provided a separate commentary on her 'control-freak' sister-in-law. A more recent gaffe in early 2008 saw colleagues wince when she suggested making a 'reverse Oreo' with black co-presenter Don Lemon and a white female colleague, then adding, 'Yeah, good times', just in case no one caught the sexual overtone.

ART FOR ART'S SAKE?

In Italy, the art schools were once hit by a nude models' strike. Protesters at La Sapienza, Rome's main university, demanded professional recognition. 'It's a tough, cold job and they do not show us much consideration,' complained 42-year-old Antonella Migliorini. 'Once a group of about thirty Japanese tourists turned up and started taking photographs.' Asked to comment, an education ministry spokesman replied, 'We need to get to the bottom of this.'

ANDY WARHOL ONE-LINERS

'Everyone will be famous for fifteen minutes.'

'An artist is someone who produces things that people don't need to have but that he - for some reason - thinks it would be a good idea to give them.'

'Don't pay any attention to what they write about you. Just measure it in inches.'

'I always wished I had died, and I still wish that, because I could have gotten the whole thing over with.'

'I had a lot of dates but I decided to
stay home and dye my eyebrows.'

'I never think that people die.
They just go to department stores.'

'It would be very glamorous to be reincarnated
as a great big ring on Liz Taylor's finger.'

GUM BLONDES

Toronto artist Jason Kronenwald creates pop portraits from masticated gum and plywood. Other, more eager, mouths do the chewing (no paints or dyes are used), while he himself works from forty to fifty hours on each portrait. Aside from a Swiss Army knife and a plastic roller, the only other tools are his fingers and thumbs. Epoxy resin is used to seal the final product. Kronenwald's series, 'Gum Blondes', includes images of Paris Hilton, Britney Spears and Brigitte Bardot.

'I think gay marriage is something that
should be between a man and a woman.'
ARNOLD SCHWARZENEGGER

BLONDE JOKES #4

A blonde walks into an electrical store and asks, 'Can I buy that TV, please?' and the shopkeeper replies, 'No, we don't sell to blondes.' So the blonde dyes her hair red and walks into the shop and asks again, 'Can I buy that TV, please?' and the shopkeeper says, 'No, we don't sell to blondes.' She then dyes her hair brown and returns to the shop and once more asks the shopkeeper if she can buy the TV and the shopkeeper repeats, 'No, we don't sell to blondes.' Puzzled, she asks, 'How do you know I'm a blonde?' And the shopkeeper replies, 'Because that's a microwave!'

*

A blonde and a brunette are walking through some woods when the brunette says, 'Oh look, clever pills!' The blonde tries one and says, 'This tastes like rabbit shit' . . . to which the brunette replies: 'See, you're getting cleverer already.'

*

A blonde is summoned to court to appear as a witness in a trial. The prosecuting barrister opens his questioning with, 'Where were you on the night of 24 August?' 'Objection! Irrelevant!' says the defence barrister. 'Oh, that's okay,' says the blonde from the witness stand. 'I don't mind answering the question.' 'I object!' says the Defence again. 'Really, I don't mind,' says the blonde. 'I'll answer.' The judge rules that there is no reason for the defence to object and so the prosecutor asks once again: 'So where were you on the night of 24 August?' The blonde replies brightly, 'I don't know!'

*

Q: Why does a blonde only change her baby's nappies once every month?
A: Because the label says: 'For up to 20 lbs.' Nice!

BUSH-ISMS

George W. Bush has had his own moments, blond or not, popularly known as Bush-isms. In a book such as this it's impossible not to include some of them:

'I can press when there needs to be pressed, I can hold hands when there needs to be . . . hold hands.'
(ON HOW HE CAN CONTRIBUTE TO THE MIDDLE EAST PEACE PROCESS)

'I don't particularly like it when
people put words in my mouth, either,
by the way, unless I say it.'

'My job is a decision-making job, and
as a result, I make a lot of decisions.'

'You helped our nation celebrate its
bicentennial in 17 . . . 1976.'
(TO THE QUEEN, MAY 2007. TO MAKE MATTERS WORSE,
AFTER ALMOST ACCUSING HER OF BEING OVER 200 YEARS OLD,
HE TURNED AND GAVE THE QUEEN A ROGUISH WINK.
IN RETURN, SHE GAVE HIM A WITHERINGLY REGAL LOOK
BUT SEEMED TO SEE THE FUNNY SIDE LATER.)

'I was never a dangerous woman. I'm not
the prissy blonde woman that could
take your husband away.'
CATHERINE DENEUVE

HAPPY BIRTHDAY

A Belarus woman had a lucky escape when she survived being run over by a high-speed train after falling asleep on the tracks following her own birthday celebration.

Svetlanda Yurkova, aged thirty-two, said, 'I'd had a few drinks and felt sleepy and just lay down on what I thought was the ground. It felt very comfortable but I later found out that it was between two rail tracks and an express train went over me during the night. I didn't even hear it. The doctors said it was a good job I was so fast asleep because otherwise I would have woken up with the sound of the train and got my head knocked off.'

Convinced she was dead, horrified onlookers had immediately called the emergency services.

POWER COUPLE

In 2007 David Beckham went blond to match his wife Victoria for a photo shoot to help launch their careers in the US. He unveiled his new look at a Real Madrid training session ahead of the photo shoot with fashion photographer Stephen Klein for *W* magazine that weekend. Teammates reportedly christened him 'Marilyn' in honour of the peroxide shade.

'We've been asked to do *Playboy* together, me and Victoria, as a pair. I don't think I'll ever go naked, but I'll never say never.'
DAVID BECKHAM

A natural golden blonde Australian went for a swim in a friend's back-yard pool. Apparently her parents had got their chlorination all wrong and the blonde emerged from the pool with lime green, waist-length hair that wouldn't wash out for weeks! End of friendship, or so I'm told.

COLEMAN (AND OTHER) BALLS

In all the excitement, sports commentators sometimes get carried away and have their own ditzy moments. And of course the male of the species often goes completely blond when it comes to the beautiful game. David Coleman was particularly prone to this and could be relied on to come up with some gems:

'That's the fastest time ever run – but it's not as fast as the world record.'

'Don't tell those coming in now the result of that fantastic match. Now let's have another look at Italy's winning goal.'

'In the Moscow Olympics, Lasse Viren came in fifth and ran a champion's race.'

Of course Coleman wasn't the only one. Here are some classics uttered by various characters from the football world . . . who then wished they hadn't:

'If you can't stand the heat in the dressing-room, get out of the kitchen.'
TERRY VENABLES

'I never make predictions and I never will.'
PAUL GASCOIGNE

'You have got to miss them to score sometimes.'
DAVE BASSETT

'Merseyside derbies usually last ninety
minutes and I'm sure today's won't be
any different.'
TREVOR BROOKING

'The game is balanced in Arsenal's favour.'
JOHN MOTSON

MALE BLONDING

During the 1998 World Cup, the entire Romanian team bleached their hair, presumably as some kind of team bonding exercise. Commentator Jimmy Hill was derided, perhaps a little unfairly, by colleagues on live TV when he suggested this might help player visibility and awareness on the pitch. In any case, the team lost to Croatia in the second round.

ONE OVER

The late Brian Johnston, much-loved cricket commentator and sports personality, was renowned for his gaffes and on-air howlers. One of his most famous moments was when he prepared listeners for the next over with a quick recap of the scene: 'The bowler's Holding, the batsman's Willey.'

In 1991 he lost his composure entirely after Jonathan Agnew described Ian Botham as missing a wicket by failing to 'get his leg over'. Johnston struggled manfully on for about thirty seconds before finally surrendering to helpless wheezy giggles.

BROOM-CUPBOARD BLUNDER

Six-times Grand Slam winner strawberry-blond Boris Becker is equally famous for his brief encounter with a Russian model. In June 1999 the German player had sex with Angela Ermakova in a broom cupboard at Nobu restaurant in London's Park Lane. Details emerged when Ermakova filed a paternity suit saying Becker was the father of her daughter, Anna. Although he at first denied it, Becker admitted paternity following DNA tests.

Becker says it all began after he lost his last match at Wimbledon. He then had a two-hour argument with his wife, Barbara (seven months pregnant at the time with their second child), which brought about the onset of labour pains (actually a false alarm). While his wife went to hospital, accompanied by a friend, Becker left their hotel room for a drink.

According to his autobiography, he had first spotted Ermakova two weeks earlier and she had given him a 'significant look': 'Now she was there again and walked past the bar twice – and again this look. Some time later she left her table and headed for the toilet. I followed her. After five minutes of small talk, we got down to business in the most convenient place.'

In February 2000 the tennis legend received a fax from Ms Ermakova in which she infrmed him that him their child was due the following month.

'I am beautiful, famous and gorgeous. I could have any man in the world.'

'The world believes all blondes are stupid and brunettes are smarter. Well, I disagree.'

ANNA KOURNIKOVA

CRICKETING HIGHLIGHTS

Graham Dilley's deeds in the 1981 and 1986–7 Ashes series represented a high point for blond English pace bowlers. While Ian Botham enjoyed a brief phase of blondness, there followed a dearth of fair-haired talent (with the exception Lancashire's Peter Martin) until the arrival of Andrew Flintoff, Matthew Hoggard and Martin Saggers.

So, might England also look to fire teams out with an all-blond pace attack? Chris Adams, then captain of Sussex, responds, 'I wouldn't have thought so. You just have to look at Johnson, Anderson and Harmison who are also in the England set-up. I hadn't really thought of this before. I suppose it must be in England that the darker you are, the more aggressive you are. But who knows? In about ten years time all us batsmen may be terrorized by blond-haired pacemen.'

SETTING THE PACE

While injuries to cricketers Glenn McGrath and Jason Gillespie may not have given Zimbabwe a better chance of saving the second Test against Australia, this paved the way for an all-blond pace attack in the shape of Brett Lee, Andy Bichel and Brad Williams. Had Williams not debuted, the only other pace-bowling option was yet another blond, Nathan Bracken. 'If my two best bowlers are out, perhaps the blonds can have some fun with the Zimbabweans?' said coach John Buchanan.

South Africa is one country that seems to have provided an excellent crop of blond pacemen, including the highly rated trio of Mike Procter, Peter Pollock and Garth Le Roux. Before his country's twenty-year international sporting exile Pollock took 116 wickets in twenty-eight Tests. Procter took 41 wickets in seven Tests at an amazing average of 15.02, while Le Roux's only taste of the big stage came courtesy of Kerry Packer. Prior to Brett Lee and Andy Bichel, you have to go back more than twenty years to find Rodney Hogg, another fair-haired bowling regular.

LAUGHING ALL THE WAY TO THE BANK

Normally measured and calculating City businessmen are not immune to their own moments of pinstriped dizziness. A chief executive of Barclays opened his mouth without thinking in 2003 when he told the press he'd never use a Barclaycard – the interest rates are too high.

'I'm in show business. I look at my boobs like they're show horses or show dogs. You have to keep them groomed.'
DOROTHY PARTON ON HER ASSETS

THE OLDEST PROFESSION

The combination of Aphrodite's lovely long blonde hair and smooth, milky hairless skin excited the ancient Greeks so much that prostitutes on earth began to mimic the Greek goddess of love, going to great lengths to dye their dark hair blonde in order to bump up business. Though peroxide hadn't yet been invented, they rubbed dye containing saffron into their hair, added highlights using coloured powders and set their curls with yellow muds. They tried every trick in the book, including (for their best customers) wigs purchased from far-off northern lands at huge expense.

According to Joanne Pitman, author of *On Blondes*, during the Crusades, boats full of prostitutes cruised up and down the Middle East and were probably staffed by French or German women with tinted blonde hair.

BOOKISH BLONDES

'Most men regard blondes as a golden opportunity.'
ANON

'She was what we used to call a suicide blonde
– dyed by her own hand.'
SAUL BELLOW

'I do a great deal of research – particularly in the apartments of tall blondes.'
RAYMOND CHANDLER

'Fair tresses man's imperial race ensnare,
And beauty draws us with a single hair.'
FROM *THE RAPE OF THE LOCK* BY ALEXANDER POPE

'Hazel Morse was a large, fair woman of the
type that incites some men when they use the
word "blonde" to click their tongues and wag
their heads roguishly.'
FROM *BIG BLONDE* BY DOROTHY PARKER

'It was a blonde. A blonde to make a bishop
kick a hole in a stained-glass window.'
FROM *FAREWELL, MY LOVELY* BY RAYMOND CHANDLER

'O Helen fair, beyond compare!
I'll make a garland of thy hair
Shall bind my heart for evermair
Until the day I die.'
'FAIR HELEN', ANON

'In Scarlet town, where I was born,
There was a fair maid dwellin',
Made every youth cry 'Well-a-way!'
Her name was Barbara Allen.'
'BARBARA ALLEN'S CRUELTY', ANON

'Yea, is not even Apollo, with hair and
harp-string of gold,
A bitter God to follow, a beautiful God to
behold?'
FROM 'HYMN TO PROSERPINE' BY A. C. SWINBURNE

'This day my wife began to wear light-coloured locks. Quite white almost, which although it made her look very pretty, yet, not being natural vexes me, that I will not have her wear them.'
SAMUEL PEPYS WRITES ABOUT HIS WIFE'S WIG IN HIS DIARY

'Lo! as that youth's eyes burned
at thine, so went
Thy spell through him, and left his
straight neck bent
And round his heart one strangling
golden hair.'
FROM 'BODY'S BEAUTY' BY DANTE GABRIEL ROSSETTI

'I can't even write a postcard.'
DARYL HANNAH

BLONDES BARD

Blonde hasn't always been the colour of the moment. In Shakespeare's *Two Gentlemen of Verona* blonde Julia compares herself to her rival in love, auburn-haired Silvia, who appears to be having all the success:

'Her hair is auburn, mine is perfect yellow:
If that be all the difference in his love,
I'll get me such a colour'd periwig.'

GIRLS IN CARS

Donna Marie Maddock, aged twenty-two, who once appeared in a Burberry bikini in the 'Chav Babes' calendar, was pulled up by police for applying her make-up with both hands while driving along a section of the A499 in North Wales, one of Britain's most dangerous roads. She told *The Sun*, 'It is what I would call one of my blonde moments. I am so blonde it is untrue when it comes to things like that. I must have looked like Penelope Pitstop driving along, slapping the make-up on, but it's something all women do – I can't see what all the fuss is about.'

*

A blonde is driving down the centre of the road at a hundred miles an hour. A police officer pulls her over and asks for her licence and registration. 'It's okay, officer, I have a special licence that allows me to do this,' she says, smiling. 'That's impossible! I've never heard of such a licence,' he replies. The blonde then reaches into her purse and hands him her licence. Astonished, the officer says, 'Just as I suspected – this is an ordinary licence. I see nothing here that allows you special consideration.' She points to the bottom of the licence: 'See? It says so right here: "Tear along the dotted line."'

*

I went to pick up my car the other day and the blond mechanic told me, 'I couldn't repair your brakes, so I just made the horn louder.'

*

Two blondes are driving through Louisiana. As they approach the town of Natchitoches, they argue over its pronunciation and they continue to argue until they stop for lunch. At the counter, one of the blondes asks the manager, 'Before we order, would you settle an argument for us? How do you pronounce the name of where we are?' The manager leans over the counter and says, 'BURRRRRR-GERRRRRRR-KIIIIIING!'

*

A blonde is having trouble with her Fiat car and she opens the hood and gasps. Another blonde, in the same type of car, stops to help. 'What's the problem?' she asks. 'Look here,' replies the first blonde. 'Someone stole my engine.' 'Relax,' says the other. 'I just checked my boot this morning and I found out that I've got a spare one. You can have it!'

THE *BIG BROTHER* BIGMOUTH

Out of all *BB* contestants, past and present, one South London girl stands out from all the rest. The inimitable Jade Goody, of course:

'The Union Jack is for all of us, but the St George is just for London, isn't it?'

'They were trying to use me as an escape goat.'

'Do they speak Portuganese in Portugal? I thought Portugal was in Spain.'

'Are they really filming us out here? I look like a state.'
(ON THE FINAL DAY IN THE GARDEN OF THE *BIG BROTHER* HOUSE)

'Rio de Janeiro, ain't that a person?'

'I am intelligent, but I let myself down because I can't speak properly or spell.'

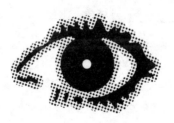

MUSICAL BLONDES

'I trip and I burp and I fart, like
everybody else.'
BRITNEY SPEARS

'Well, I lost my virginity in a car
but it wasn't a very nice one.'
BRITTANY MURPHY

'Pre-1989, I pretty much f**ked everybody.
I had to get breakfast somehow!'
COURTNEY LOVE

'I've always said that if I hadn't been
a woman, then I'd have damn sure been
a drag queen!'
DOLLY PARTON

'I'm not some blonde bimbo. I want to
be a successful businesswoman.'
SARAH HARDING, MEMBER OF GIRL-BAND GIRLS ALOUD

WIG WHAMMY

In 2007 Britney Spears wandered about in a glamorous blonde wig. Just the day before she made headlines by shaving off her own hair during an impromptu visit to a Los Angeles hairdresser, while fans looked on through the windows. She reportedly checked into rehab, checked out again within twenty-four hours and then relinquished her naturally blonde locks.

Professor Cary Cooper, expert on stress at Lancaster University, said: 'I think it's a call for help. She's saying, "I'm very confused, I'm not in control at the moment; I need a fresh start, I need help." We take these young kids and turn them into celebrities, but they don't necessarily have the infrastructure to help them deal with the pressures they are going to face.'

In April 2008 Britney reportedly asked her former manager to get her personal and professional life back on course. She is tipped for her own TV show and has also been offered a job as receptionist for animal-rights group PETA.

MORE FAQS ABOUT BLONDES

Q: What do clever blondes and dinosaurs have
in common?
A: They're both extinct.

Q: Why did the blonde stare at the carton of
orange juice?
A: It said concentrate.

Q: Why did the blonde cross the road?
A: I have no idea – and neither does she.

Q: What do you call a blonde with a leather jacket?
A: Rebel without a clue.

SHE WAS *SO* BLONDE . . .

* she put lipstick on her forehead because she wanted
to make up her mind

* when she heard that 90 per cent of all crimes occur
around the home, she moved

* when she missed the 44 bus, she took the 22
twice instead

* at the bottom of her application, where it said 'sign
here', she simply wrote 'Sagittarius'.

PETS' CORNER

One day in 1986, keen to acquire some pets, former Nirvana frontman Kurt Cobain went out and purchased half a dozen turtles. He then placed them in a bathtub in the middle of his living room. All was well until the stench of turtle excrement became overpowering. His solution was simply to drill a drainage hole . . . right in the middle of the living-room floor.

'There are assumptions made about the way you look. I'm always surprised when people don't think I'm smart.'
MEG RYAN

AMERICAN BEAUTY

'How did you guys run so slowly in that
opening *Baywatch* scene . . . you know,
where you're running down the beach?'
(ON MEETING PAMELA ANDERSON)

'I kinda want to be the Reese Witherspoon of
the music industry . . . the girl-next-door who
wears a great dress and has great hair.'

'Everybody is a dumb blonde at heart.'

JESSICA SIMPSON

OLD CHINESE PROVERB SAY . . .

David Beckham has a tattoo running from his left nipple
down to his groin. But *what* does it mean? It seems
the phrase is a Chinese proverb and roughly translates
as, 'Death and life have their determined appointment.
Riches and honour depend on Heaven.' But what does
that mean? A 'source' provided enlightenment – of sorts:
'The latest tattoo uses a completely different technique
to all the others. It appears on his skin as if it has been
brushed on. It is a really intricate process and unique to

Hong Kong. He has always wanted the Chinese brush-stroke effect. Victoria loves it. There is more emphasis on the word life – which is in bold ink, with the word death slightly smaller. The proverb has strong meaning for David. He is really thoughtful about the tattoos he gets. He doesn't just rush in.'

Perhaps not, but there's no denying Becks is beginning to run out of space. A month earlier he revealed a tattoo on his left forearm that reads: 'forever by your side'. Often the case with arms, surely?

CELEBRITY STYLE

'Doesn't that hurt?'
ANNA NICOLE SMITH ON SUICIDE BOMBERS

'I can't wait to dye my hair back to blonde –
it's about time people saw the real Abi
and stopped messing me about.'
ABI TITMUSS, GLAMOUR MODEL TURNED TV PRESENTER

'Well, I paid for it, so I guess I get to keep it.
It will go in the archive somewhere.'
MARTHA STEWART ON HER SECURITY TAG

IT'S MY PARTY . . .

At the height of his fame, peroxide blond Generation X star Billy Idol caused $140,000 worth of damage while partying in a penthouse suite in Thailand. (He claimed he could get any drug he wanted out there.) Unsurprisingly, he was asked to leave. When he refused, Thai soldiers swiftly tied the rebel musician to a stretcher and escorted him from the country.

Did you know?
The name 'Billy Idol' is a play on a teacher's school report card, which read, 'William is idle.'

THE MALE OF THE SPECIES

So, does the male blond relish or simply endure his uniqueness? You decide:

'I was just really concerned that I had not been getting enough publicity. I wanted to do something to draw more attention.'
BRAD PITT EXPLAINS WHY HE BLEACHED HIS HAIR BLOND

'If you're as blond as I am, and you have blond
lashes, you have to wear mascara, otherwise
you're invisible on stage.'
MICHAEL CAINE'S SECRET WEAPON

'Don't do drugs, don't have unprotected sex,
don't be violent ... Leave that to me.'
EMINEM

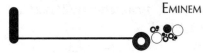

KISS-AND-TELL STORY

On the set of *The Electric Horseman* in 1979, Robert
Redford and Jane Fonda were shooting a tender kissing
scene. The director was Sydney Pollock, who was famed
for his perfectionism. Between 9 a.m. on a Tuesday and 6
p.m. the next day, he ordered forty-eight takes – at a cost
of $280,000. Unamused, the studio accountant wryly
remarked, 'It would have been cheaper if Redford had
kissed the horse.'

'Every relationship I've been in, I've overwhelmed the girl. They just can't handle all the love.'

'The advantages are that you don't get in as many arguments, and the disadvantage is that you're talking to yourself.'

(ON THE PLUSES AND MINUSES OF NOT BEING IN A RELATIONSHIP)

'This is only my first album, so stick with me – we've got depression and drug addiction to go through.'

JUSTIN TIMBERLAKE

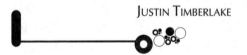

ICE-COOL BLOND

Five-times Wimbledon champion Bjorn Borg, who retired from tennis having turned just twenty-five, was always an ice-blond enigma, but this story shows he has a kind heart. In 1981, a teenager wearing the same Fila outfit made famous by Borg approached him nervously. He had created a collage of Borg pictures and hoped his hero might be suitably impressed and autograph his work.

As Borg headed for the clubhouse after a two-hour practice session, the boy quickly walked up to him, showed him the collage and handed him a pen, saying, 'Mr Borg, please!' Borg stopped, looked at the work, smiled and asked, 'You made this?' The boy simply nodded. Borg signed and said, 'I should get *your* autograph for preparing this,' patted him on the shoulder and walked on.

That same boy, now in his early forties, still has the collage and remembers catching a glimpse of a true sportsman.

THE BLONDE JOKE TO END ALL BLONDE JOKES . . .

A girl was visiting her blonde friend who had recently acquired two new dogs and she asked what their names were. The blonde responded by saying that one was called Rolex and the other was named Timex. Her friend paused and then said, 'Whoever heard of someone giving dogs names like that?'

'Hellooooo . . .' replied the blonde. 'They're *watch* dogs!'

THE DUTCH PAUL NEWMAN

> 'I don't know what the appeal is. I can see
> I've got blue eyes and I don't look like
> the Hunchback of Notre Dame but I can't
> understand the fuss.'
> RUTGER HAUER

Blond, blue-eyed and handsome, Dutch actor Rutger Hauer (b. 1944) has played everything from romantic leads to action heroes and sinister villains. He is famous for his role in the 1982 sci-fi thriller *Blade Runner* and his humorous appearances in commercials for Guinness. At the age of fifteen he ran away from home to work on a freight ship for a year but, fortunately for his fans, colour-blindness prevented him from furthering his career as a sailor.

'God is a gentleman. He prefers blondes.'
FROM THE PLAY *LOOT*, BY JOE ORTON,

BLONDE REALLY *IS* AN ATTITUDE

Mary Louise Cecilia 'Texas' Guinan (1884–1933) was a saloon keeper, entrepreneur and became the world's first movie cowgirl, nicknamed 'The Queen of the West' when she appeared in the silent movie *The Wildcat* in 1917. In addition to her film career, she also entertained the troops in France during World War I.

A month before her death, she neatly described herself in the *Dallas Morning News* on 6 November 1933: 'I like noise, rhinestone heels, customers, plenty of attention and red velvet bathing suits. I smoke like a five-alarm fire. I eat an aspirin every night before I go to bed. I call every man I don't know "Fred" and they love it. I have six uncles. I sleep on my right side. I like carrots. I eat a dozen oranges every day and I once took off thirty-five pounds in two weeks. I guess that settles my personality . . .'

DURING THE COURSE
OF RESEARCH

From: Mel
To: Fleur Barrington
Subject: Brunette moment

Hi Fleur,

Lovely to hear from you and I will certainly give this some thought, but having slipped two disks in my back, I'm on pretty wacky pain relief at the moment and thinking is not in my top 10! I managed to have a brunette moment last summer when I thought I would put a little superglue on my kitchen floor to secure a loose tile. I put my foot down to make sure it stuck, didn't allow for overspill and ended up literally glued in one place! Thank goodness I could still reach the kettle, the sink, my mobile . . .

Would love to meet up soon and will be in touch. Hope all is well with you and much love,

Mel xxx

From: Jason
To: Fleur Barrington
Subject: Blonde moment?

Fleur,

You know what, I've been racking my brain all weekend and I just can't think of any blonde moments. I mean, I know that I have had many in my life, quite funny moments, but I just can't seem to find them.

So, I'm in an Internet cafe with a friend, telling him that I can't think of any, and he thinks this is a blonde moment. Is it?

Jason

ACKNOWLEDGEMENTS

I would like to thank Louise Dixon at Michael O'Mara Books for asking me to write this book and for her encouragement and enthusiasm for the project. Also Kerry Chapple and Michael O'Mara for their invaluable contribution, and the designer Ana Bjezancevic and illustrator Paul Moran for bringing my words to life in such brilliant style. Thanks to Lesley Levene for recommending me to Louise and to Conrad Barrington and Edel Kelleher for a fine selection of blonde jokes, David Lloyd for sharing his knowledge of football, Jane Forster for pointing me in the direction of *Two Gentlemen of Verona*, Sandra Rigby for the swimming-pool story and Becky Luckens, Celia Rumley and Caroline Sangster for sharing their own blonde moments with me over a girls' weekend (and to Louise Turpin and Ros Shakibi for reminding me to write it all down!). I am very grateful to Melanie Letts and Jason Filby for allowing me to reproduce their wonderful emails. Thanks also to Boris Johnson for providing such a wealth of material.

Finally, I would like to thank Shaun Barrington for reading the manuscript and for his inspired suggestions; also for tolerating some of my blondest moments. This book is for you, with all my love.